# JIMI HENDRIX

## THE MAN, THE MUSIC, THE MEMORABILIA

### CAESAR GLEBEEK & DOUGLAS J. NOBLE

## THUNDER'S MOUTH PRESS

NEW YORK

Published in North America by Thunder's Mouth Press
632 Broadway, Seventh Floor
New York, New York 10012

First published by Dragon's World Ltd 1996

Library of Congress Catalog Number: 96-60077

ISBN 1-56025-099-2

EDITOR:               Jane Hurd-Cosgrave
ART DIRECTOR:         John Strange
COVER DESIGN:         Mel Raymond
DESIGN:               Peter Bridgewater Design Co.
EDITORIAL DIRECTOR:   Pippa Rubinstein

**A Note to the Reader**

Although attempts have been made to trace copyright holders of images contained herein, any
unacknowledged copyright holder omitted should contact the publisher so that the situation may
be rectified in future editions.
   Neither the authors nor publishers of this book condone the manufacture, distribution or sale of
so-called bootleg recordings. The bootlegging of material belonging to any group or individual is
strictly  illegal. The bootlegs in this book are included solely for the purpose of historical accuracy.

Printed in Italy by Amadeus S.p.A. - Rome

# Contents

*CG*
**Dedicated to Jimi Hendrix and Richard Thompson admirers around the globe!**

*DJN*
**Dedicated to all my guitar pupils!**

# FOREWORD

Personally, I think that the clothes and hairstyles of the Jimi Hendrix Experience (apart from the music) really helped in our success. We were *there* in London when the Kings Road/Carnaby Street fashion thing was 'in', and we were part of it.

Before you sit down with this book, which illustrates the complete history of the (now legendary) Jimi Hendrix Experience, allow me to tell you an anecdote about the time we played at 'The Empire' in Liverpool on 9 April 1967. The day after our two shows, there was going to be a circus a bit further down the road from the venue. In between our shows, Jimi and I visited a pub next door to 'The Empire'. I ordered two pints, but the bartender flatly refused to serve us – instead, he said 'Clowns aren't allowed in here!', and showed us the way out....

*– Noel Redding*

# INTRODUCTION

My love for music originated from my late father, but we didn't admire the same kind of material – he would listen to the BBC for their *Sing Something Simple* transmissions while I would tune in to Radio Luxembourg and Radio Caroline. That's where I first heard the Jimi Hendrix Experience single 'Hey Joe' in December 1966. Pocket money was a joke in those days, so most evenings were devoted to taping interesting singles (LP tracks were rarely played at the time) on a 5" reel-to-reel recorder. DJs who talked over songs were not popular in our house! Since accurate information on pop musicians was very hard to come by in those years (I recall a guy claiming on the radio that Jimi Hendrix was 'an eskimo'!), I would trot off into the centre of Amsterdam every Saturday and read music papers for hours non-stop. If they carried reasonably sized articles on Jimi Hendrix I would buy a copy, thus starting my collection of Hendrix memorabilia. In May 1967, I bought my very first LP, a mono copy of *Are You Experienced?* It had to be replaced several times as scratches would make the LP totally unplayable after a while.

Almost thirty years later, my Hendrix collection has grown considerably, and a good portion of those artefacts are on display in this book. Don't get me wrong, though – I am not one of those collectors who want to own everything that's out there in memorabilia-land – my interest in Jimi Hendrix is primarily in his music.

I have been fortunate enough to see Jimi Hendrix perform live in concert several times, and I've made friends with fellow Hendrix lovers all over the world. As one of the few true musical visionaries of this century, Jimi Hendrix continues to touch souls and brighten up many people's lives. Enjoy!

*– Caesar Glebbeek*

# THE EARLY YEARS

"Music is very serious to me. Other people
may think it's a load of junk or senseless,
but it's my way of saying what I want to say."

*Jimi Hendrix*

**D**iscovered by mountain lions who put him on an eagle's back, Jimi Hendrix was flown past the outskirts of infinity and given the Venus witch's ring.... Jimi Hendrix made a myth of his birth on his double LP *Electric Ladyland*, reinventing himself as a 'Voodoo Child' and singing of supernatural phenomena. However, the reality surrounding Jimi's birth was far more mundane.

### BEGINNING

Johnny Allen Hendrix, as his mother Lucille named him, was born in Seattle on 27 November 1942. Like the woman Lucille in Little Richard's later rock 'n' roll classic of the same name, Jimi's

▲ **Jimi (at eight months old) with his grandmother, Clarice Jeter.**
*Seattle, July 1943*

mother was a free spirit. 'We met at a friend's house...' and 'went to a dance that night...,' remembered Jimi's father, Al Hendrix. Al and Lucille shared a love of dancing, and their relationship quickly blossomed – Lucille became pregnant, and the couple were married. Only seventeen and in a delicate state of health when Jimi was born, Lucille Hendrix was way too young to settle down and raise a family. To make matters worse, Al had been drafted into the US army, and was denied leave to visit his wife and new-born son because his unit was preparing to serve overseas.

Lucille had no home of her own and very little money – thanks to an administrative error by the army that delayed her receiving help from Al – so she and the baby moved in with a friend of her sister's, but they soon had to move out again as there wasn't enough room. Lucille and Jimi were then forced to live in a succession of dingy hotels until Lucille's mother, Clarice Jeter, came to help them after her husband died. Lucille worked as a waitress, and Mrs. Jeter got a job as a housemaid for a local family, the Maes.

'Oh Jimi, you poor little angel!' was the Mae family's reaction to the frequently abandoned infant. They took pity on Jimi's situation, and would often look after him, so Jimi was passed around between Lucille, Mrs. Jeter and the Maes. Now that Lucille had people to babysit Jimi she was free to spend nights on the town, and sometimes wouldn't be seen for days at a time. Occasionally, Lucille would take Jimi around the country as she travelled with her boyfriend, John Williams ('Williams' is not his real surname) – although she was married, this didn't stop Lucille doing whatever she wanted. However, as much as Lucille enjoyed her freedom, she often suffered in her relationships, and on one occasion was hospitalized after Williams beat her up.

▲ **Lucille Hendrix, Jimi's mother.**
*Seattle, 1948*

Not surprisingly, the transient lifestyle eventually took its toll on Jimi's health, and he fell ill with pneumonia. A friend of Mrs. Jeter's, Mrs. Champ, offered to look after Jimi, so he moved from Seattle to Berkeley to live with her. As she was able to offer some much-needed stability in the baby's life, Mrs. Champ wrote to Al saying that she thought it would be best for Jimi to stay with her and her family.

▲ **Jimi posing for a photographer.**
*Seattle, 15 January 1946*

▲ **A picture of the young Jimi was featured on the cover of *Esquire* magazine (Japan) in 1993.**
*Seattle, mid 1946*

As Jimi approached his third birthday, Al was stationed in the Fiji Islands. After receiving his discharge papers in November 1945, Al travelled by train up to Berkeley to collect his son. As a precaution, Al had obtained a copy of Jimi's birth certificate, since Mrs. Champ had made it clear that she was not willing to hand Jimi back to Al, even though she had no legal right to him. Mrs. Champ was forced to give the baby up, and Al brought Jimi back to Seattle. When Lucille heard that Al was back in town, they set up a happy home together. According to Lucille's sister, Delores, 'It was like they were on honeymoon'. Al and Lucille would often go out dancing together, and for the first time in his life, Jimi enjoyed the love and stability of a traditional two-parent family.

Lucille had not consulted Al about Jimi's name. Al objected to 'Johnny Allen' because it reminded him of John Williams, so he changed Jimi's name to James Marshall Hendrix. In January 1948, the Hendrixes had another son, Leon Morris Hendrix, but Lucille continued to be torn between domesticity with her family and wild times with her drinking buddies. The strain on the marriage proved too much – Al and Lucille separated, and finally divorced in December 1951. The lack of emotional stability in his early years meant that Jimi retreated into himself and became very shy, a trait that never completely left him. Jimi later referred to his parents' turbulent marriage in his song '51st Anniversary', the flip side of the 'Purple Haze' single from March 1967: 'So now you're seventeen...,' sang Jimi, Lucille being seventeen when she married, 'Life for you has just begun....'

Al was granted custody of Jimi and Leon, although the two boys would still see their mother from time to time. When Jimi began school, his early reports showed him to be best at art and sports, although generally below average in other subjects, including – surprisingly – music. Already showing a vivid youthful imagination, Jimi would paint scenes of Martian landscapes and pretend to be the character Flash Gordon as he played in the streets around his home. 'Flash Gordon' was Jimi's favourite film, and he was nicknamed 'Buster' after actor Buster Crabbe, who played Flash Gordon in the popular Hollywood sci-fi films.

Back in the real world, Al struggled to pay the bills, working long hours at menial jobs that paid very little money. Leon was almost constantly fostered out, living with nine different foster families altogether, although Jimi and Leon were able to see each other during the school summer holidays.

Meanwhile, Lucille's always-delicate health had been getting worse, and on 2 February 1958 she suffered a fatal haemorrhage. Jimi was grief-stricken by his mother's death, and found it difficult to express himself – his unstable upbringing had taught him to hide his emotions. However, he was beginning to discover a release for all the pain and confusion inside him: music.

## HEAR MY GUITAR A'COMIN'

Jimi had grown up surrounded by music, from the dance music his parents played at home to the songs he sang in the Pentecostal Church with Mrs. Jeter. As his love for music grew, Jimi would pretend to play the guitar, using a broom and singing the notes he imagined he was making. His obsession grew to such a degree that the social worker at Horace Mann Elementary School which Jimi attended saw that it was actually damaging for Jimi not to have a guitar, and asked the school to buy him one. Unfortunately, this was to no avail, as the special school fund was for important items like clothes and shoes, not 'play' things like guitars! Eventually, Al bought Jimi an acoustic guitar from a friend for five dollars. 'I wanted something I could carry with me, and I couldn't carry a piano around,' said Jimi.

Although Jimi wrote with his right hand, his natural inclination was to play guitar left-handed. He took the strings off the guitar and put them on the other way round for left-handed playing: 'It was way out of tune when I finished. I didn't know a thing about tuning, so I went to the store and ran my fingers across the strings on a guitar they had there. After that I was able to tune my own.' Unlike most beginners who have a great deal of difficulty tuning the guitar, Jimi, with his innately musical ear, found it quite easy.

'When I was fifteen, I decided the guitar was the instrument for me,' Jimi later said of his chosen instrument. He quickly became a competent player, learning by ear from the radio and records. At last he had an outlet for the emotions bottled up inside him. Fascinated by gadgets and technology, Jimi became desperate to get an electric guitar. Finally, he persuaded Al to take him to Myers Music Store in downtown Seattle, where he got his first electric guitar, a Supro Ozark. Al bought a saxophone so that they could play together, and succeeded in establishing a real point of contact with his son.

Jimi soon found himself in his first proper band, the Rocking Kings. Although Al's financial position meant Jimi didn't have an amplifier of his own, the band's rehearsals gave Jimi regular access to an amp. At this stage, Jimi was playing bass parts on his guitar while the lead guitar parts were played by Ulysses Heath. Keen to broaden his knowledge of the guitar, Jimi would learn from Ulysses and everyone else he heard, including all the popular sax players and R&B musicians of the day, particularly bluesmen such as Muddy Waters.

▲ **Jimi posing with his red-painted Danelectro guitar, Seattle, 1961. The night before this shot was taken, Jimi did a gig with The Tom Cats – bandleader Perry Thomas charged Jimi $5.00 for the red jacket!**

*Seattle, 1961*

Searetha Green

Willie Hailey

Dave Hampton

Willia Hartfield

James Hendrix

Corrie Hirano*

▲ **Jimi with some of his fellow students from Garfield High School.**

*Seattle, 1960*

In the spring of 1960, the Rocking Kings won second prize in the All State Band of the Year contest for Washington State, and they started a three-night-a-week residency at the Birdland club in Seattle. Then one night at the Birdland club, disaster struck – Jimi's guitar was stolen. He had left his guitar on the bandstand unattended, and when he returned it was gone. Jimi was stunned – not only had he lost his most important possession, but how would he tell Al? His father would be furious at Jimi's carelessness, especially when money was so tight.

Eventually, Jimi plucked up the courage to tell Al. 'You're gonna have to do without a guitar for a while,' Al told him. But Jimi was so distressed at not having a guitar that his aunt, Mary Hendrix, bought him a new one – a Danelectro.

As Jimi's confidence grew, he began to assert his individuality by painting his guitar red and decorating it with feathers. Keen for new musical experiences, Jimi would jam with other bands all over Seattle. On one occasion when he didn't have his guitar with him, he asked to borrow another guitarist's instrument – which happened to be a right-handed one. Thinking that Jimi wouldn't be able to play it, the band's guitarist lent Jimi his guitar and stood aside expecting Jimi to fall flat on his face. Much to his chagrin, Jimi coolly picked up the guitar and played it as if he were a right-hander.

Jimi's obvious talent led to resentment from other jealous musicians, but helped his band to get better gigs. Playing at Cottage Lake in the summer of 1960, the Rocking Kings performed in front of their biggest audience yet: over 2,000 people. Jimi rose to the occasion, and entertained the crowd by playing the guitar behind his head and between his legs – traditional techniques used by the more flamboyant blues guitarists of the time, which were later to become part of Jimi's world-famous stage act.

Although they were beginning to get better exposure, some of the band grew tired of putting up with the hassles of badly paid gigs and left. The remaining Rocking Kings members reformed with a slightly different line-up, changing their name to The Tom Cats. As the new line-up included a bass player, Jimi was released from playing bass parts, and was free to develop more of his own personal style.

As Jimi became more obsessed with music, his school work fell behind – something Al had always feared. Obviously, Jimi's education wasn't helped by the many changes of school he had as he and Al moved through ten different addresses. In October 1960, Jimi left Garfield High School without graduating, the school citing 'work referral and age' as the reasons for his leaving. Jimi gave a different reason, though: 'I had a girlfriend in art classes, and we used to hold hands all the time. The art teacher didn't dig that at all. She was very prejudiced. I said, "What, are you jealous?" She started crying and I got thrown out.'

Jimi started looking for a job, but he had no luck. As Al said, 'That was before the civil rights thing, and it was hard for blacks to get into certain jobs.' Al had finally found regular work as a landscape gardener, so Jimi started working with his dad. Sadly, the Hendrix partnership was doomed to failure – Jimi hated carting stones and cement around people's gardens, and was even convinced that Al was ripping him off for the work he was doing.

Jimi's unstable upbringing might have left him insecure and shy, but his guitar playing bolstered his confidence enough for him to stand up for himself – occasionally in a rebellious sense. Although he wasn't a particularly troublesome adolescent, Jimi's love of fancy clothes led him into trouble. Having little money to dress the way he wanted, Jimi and a friend broke into a clothes shop once. Inevitably, though, their conscience got the better of them – or perhaps they thought they were going to get caught – and they returned the clothes. Luckily for Jimi, the owner of the clothes shop decided not to press charges. It wasn't his only brush with the law, though – Jimi was caught taking a car without permission, then only days later, he was again arrested for riding in a stolen car. 'I never knew it was stolen!' he protested, but his plea fell on deaf ears. He spent seven days in jail, and was given a two-year suspended sentence – the judge decided to be lenient since Jimi was considering joining the army as a paratrooper. Jimi saw no other option – all Seattle seemed to offer him was bad memories and no future, particularly for a young black man without a high school diploma (in those days, joining the army was about the only 'respectable' option open to a young man in Jimi's position). So when Jimi went off to join the army at the age of nineteen, for the first time in his life he would be able to 'leave it all behind'.

▲ **Extremely rare booth-photo of Jimi (right) and an army pal known as 'Tutti'.**
*Fort Campbell, Kentucky, early 1962*

## UP FROM THE SKIES

'Machine gun, tearin' my body apart/Evil man make me kill you,' sang Jimi in 'Machine Gun' with the Band of Gypsys in December 1969. Hardly the sentiments 'Uncle Sam' would expect from his clean-cut defenders of the flag! But at this early stage in his life, Jimi was a patriot, and believed in the might and right of the USA. And nothing in his training as a parachuting 'Screamin' Eagle' was designed to enlighten recruits as to the more complex and sinister realities of the world's political stage, later to become evident in the widely protested US involvement in Vietnam.

Surprisingly, when Jimi left Seattle in May 1961, he didn't take his guitar with him, although he was possibly waiting to see how safe it would be, having learnt his lesson earlier when his first electric guitar was stolen. Jimi kept his guitar playing up by borrowing guitars from around the army camp and otherwise continued his habit of pretending to play guitar when he didn't have one. Finally, he asked Al to send him his guitar.

Jimi had always had a healthy streak of individuality in his youth and had been regarded as a bit of an outsider. Now in the army, Jimi stood out even more. What kind of a weirdo was this who slept with his guitar? his colleagues wondered. An explanation for this seemingly bizarre piece of behavior would no doubt have been wasted on most of his army buddies, but Jimi was merely continuing a blues tradition which expressed love and commitment to the instrument, and also made the guitar harder to steal.

Jimi's continual playing was overheard by a fellow paratrooper called Billy Cox, who described what he heard as 'a cross between Beethoven and John Lee Hooker.' A keen bass player, Billy introduced himself to Jimi. Billy's solid

— Taken
Feb 22, 196

Here's a picture that
I took dureing one of the
snowy times – I wasn't
on this jump – we went
down to the drop zone and
watched them jump –
this is right before
he touched –
when he did, he
hit with a splat –

Jimmy H.

March 5, 1962

▲ **Jimi's photo and report from 'Jumpschool'!**

*Fort Campbell, 22 February 1962*

bass work reflected his dependable, down-to-earth personality, and perfectly complemented Jimi's expansive playing style. Soon they had formed a band called the King Kasuals, and were playing in and around the army base. But just as Jimi's attention to his school work had wavered as he started to play gigs, so did his enthusiasm for the army begin to wane once he got involved in the band.

Instead of defending the free world against the oppressive forces of a foreign power, Jimi found himself with rather less heroic tasks. 'The army really taught me what boredom is. There's nothing more monotonous than spending a whole day peeling potatoes!' Even so, Jimi still gained his Screamin' Eagle patch, and was even promoted to Private First Class. Then, 'One day, I got my ankle caught in the sky-hook just as I was going to jump, and I broke it. I told them I hurt my back too. Every time they examined me I groaned, so they finally believed me and I got out.'

Initially intending to return to Seattle, Jimi ran out of money to get home, and so he waited near the army base until Billy got out as well. The two of them decided to try their luck at playing music together in and around Nashville, and formed another incarnation of the King Kasuals. They ended up playing many dismal, badly paying gigs. One night, however, Jimi was spotted by an aspiring guitarist, who introduced himself as Larry Lee. Jimi was more than willing to show the novice Larry some of his licks, but Larry couldn't have possibly imagined that, seven years later, he would be taking the stage with Jimi at the Woodstock festival in front of some 35,000 people!

Playing in the backing band for visiting musicians such as Carla Thomas and Nappy Brown helped to keep Jimi's body and soul together. Larry Lee got Jimi a gig playing with Bob Fisher and The Barnevilles, touring with the Marvellettes and Curtis Mayfield. Jimi was allowed to use Mayfield's gear – it was the first time he had been able to use good equipment, and he tested it to the limits, blowing up Mayfield's amp in the process!

When the tour was over, Jimi ended up back in Nashville, and realised he had to sharpen up his playing even more to stand out from the crowd. As Jimi later said, 'It was one of the hardest audiences in the South. They hear it all the time – everybody knows how to play guitar. You walk down the street and people are sitting on the porch playing more guitar. That's where I learned to play, really – Nashville.' But Nashville was also where he almost stopped singing – after backing many fine singers, Jimi had become very self-conscious about his voice, and wouldn't sing if he could avoid it.

Jimi got a gig playing guitar for a flamboyant singer/MC/valet/promoter called 'Gorgeous' George Odell, and then spent the next two years 'paying his dues' on the southern 'chitlin' circuit'. Frustrated with bad pay and endless one-night stands, Jimi returned to Nashville to see his old friends. 'We were playing at the Baron,' recalled Larry Lee. 'This promoter told Jimi that he had seen him play, and that he could get anything he wanted if he would go back to New York [with him]. He could get Jimi top money....' As Jimi was going nowhere in Nashville, he decided he might as well take the plunge, so he set off for New York City.

### SIDEMAN CITY

On the way to New York, Jimi broke his journey up by stopping off in Philadelphia, where he was hired to record with saxophonist Lonnie Youngblood. Youngblood's single 'Go Go Shoes' b/w 'Go Go Place', released in America in late 1963, became Jimi's first record release. Encouraged by this experience, Jimi's optimism was soon dashed when he arrived in the Big Apple to find that the promises of the promoter had come to nothing, leaving Jimi stranded with no money and no work.

Looking for a gig in the Palm Café, Jimi met a woman called Fay Pridgeon, an ex-girlfriend of singer Sam Cooke. Attracted by Jimi's innocent looks and soft voice, Fay took Jimi back to her mother's place for food then back to a hotel for sex. They started living together in Harlem, and Jimi struggled to get gigs, quickly finding that New York was little better than Nashville for yet another unknown guitar player.

Then one night in the Palm Café, Jimi was spotted by a friend of the Isley Brothers, a successful touring and recording outfit who were looking for a guitarist. Jimi was asked to audition, and was offered the job – his first major break. Jimi played on their 'Testify' single (1964) and went on tour with them. Unlike many of the musicians Jimi had backed previously, the Isleys gave Jimi more space to do his own thing, both musically and visually.

The road with the Isleys eventually led back to Seattle. Unfortunately, Jimi disappeared with an old girlfriend and ended up missing the tour bus the next day. Even worse, his guitar was stolen again. A lesser musician would have been sacked on the spot, but it says much for the Isley Brothers' opinion of Jimi that they not only took him back, but also got him a Fender Duosonic, the first Fender guitar Jimi owned.

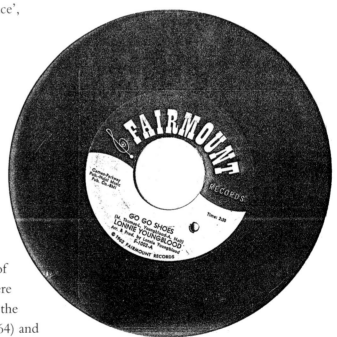

▲ The first single, 'Go Go Shoes' by Lonnie Youngblood, that Jimi ever played guitar on.

▲ Jimi (playing a Fender Duosonic guitar) during a gig with the Isley Brothers.
*USA, 1964*

▼ The only Little Richard single, released in November 1965, which featured Jimi.

The Isley Brothers were good employers to work for, but Jimi eventually grew tired of being a hired gun expected to do the will of his masters. As they drove through Nashville on tour, Jimi decided to quit the band, hopping off the bus to return to his earlier musical hunting grounds. Shortly afterwards, Jimi met Steve Cropper, the house guitarist for the Stax record label's band, who had had a hit with 'Green Onions' as Booker T and the MGs in 1962. Jimi said he wanted to record a song, so Cropper obligingly helped him with the technicalities in a nearby studio. Sadly, the demo was never released, and was probably destroyed long ago, but Jimi appreciated Cropper's help and encouragement at the time.

Jimi returned to working with Gorgeous George, and ended up playing guitar for Little Richard – he had previously jammed with Little Richard's backing band, who were already aware of his prodigious talent. In between gigging and recording with Little Richard, Jimi met Arthur Lee (founder of the group 'Love') in Los Angeles, who asked Jimi to play on a recording of a song called 'My Diary' that he had written for a singer called Rosa Lee Brooks. Jimi mimicked Curtis Mayfield's guitar style for 'My Diary' (1965), something he also did for Little Richard's single, 'I Don't Know What You've Got But It's Got Me' (1965). Musically, it was a strange time for Jimi – just as he was beginning to get his own sound together, he was being called on to play like Curtis Mayfield as back-up for other artists!

Although Jimi was gaining valuable experience, things did not go well with Little Richard. The star of the show made it clear that no-one in his band was going to upstage him, either musically or visually, and the money didn't turn out to be too good either. 'He didn't pay us for about five and a half weeks, and you can't live on promises when you're on the road – so I had to cut that mess aloose,' Jimi wrote to his father, later summing up his Little Richard period with, 'Bad pay, lousy living and getting burned.'

After he split from Little Richard, Jimi went back to living with Fay Pridgeon again in New York, where he bought Bob Dylan's sixth album, *Highway 61 Revisited* (1965). Dylan's potent and innovative mixture of folk, rock 'n' roll and surreal imagery was changing the course of rock music, and Jimi was an immediate convert. 'You must admire that guy for having that much nerve to sing so out of key,' thought Jimi. Still very self-conscious about his voice after he had toured with singers such as Curtis Mayfield and the Isley Brothers, Dylan's highly individual singing style showed that a singer needn't have 'beautiful pipes' to carry a song. Perhaps Jimi could sing after all! Dylan's music inspired Jimi to move to Greenwich Village in New York City – the 'happening' place of the time – as Jimi sensed that he might be accepted into the free-thinking, open-minded artistic community the Village was known for. As Fay didn't want to join him, he left her behind while he moved yet again, thinking that maybe this time, he would finally find what he was looking for.

In Autumn 1965, Jimi met singer Curtis Knight in New York City. Knight had his own band, the Squires, who were recording with producer Ed Chalpin. Jimi and Knight were keen to jam together, but Jimi had pawned his guitar, so Knight lent him one. Back in Jimi's hotel room, Knight was stunned by Jimi's guitar playing. Sensing he had stumbled upon a rare talent, Knight took Jimi to meet Chalpin. And Chalpin immediately realized he could make use of Jimi's talent....

## TAKING CARE OF NO BUSINESS

The first thing a starving musician ought to do when offered a contract is to consult a good lawyer, but in practice, finding the next meal and a roof to sleep under usually take precedence over legal matters.

Chalpin signed Jimi to PPX Enterprises to 'produce and play and/or sing exclusively for PPX' for three years. In return, Jimi got... Very little. PPX would pay Jimi the absolute minimum fee for sessions and a 1% royalty – after PPX had deducted expenses, naturally. All in all, a very bad deal, but Jimi had very little experience of business matters, and he willingly signed. It wasn't long before he bitterly regretted it.

Jimi started gigging and recording with Curtis Knight and the Squires, but, as he was always looking for something better, he auditioned for sax player King Curtis. A respected session player who had played with many great musicians, King Curtis recognized talent when he saw it, and immediately hired Jimi. Yet again, it was the same old story – Jimi was expected to do the band leader's bidding for only a few dollars. Understandably, Jimi soon left.

▼ **Hard-to-find original Curtis Knight single on RSVP from late 1965/early 1966.**

Things were no better back with Curtis Knight. Jimi was miserable, but couldn't leave because he was using Knight's guitar. Seeing how unhappy he was, Jimi's new girlfriend Carol Shiroky bought Jimi his first Fender Stratocaster. Since Jimi had always found left-handed guitars hard to come by, he had grown accustomed to using right-handed models with the strings reversed. As to his performing – Jimi reckoned that if he was miserable and starving while playing for other people, things could be no worse if he formed his own band. So, he renamed himself Jimmy James and found some other musicians to play with him in the first band of his own – Jimmy James and the Blue Flames.

▲ **Jimi (on a Fender Duosonic) gigging with Curtis Knight & The Squires.**

*New York City, late 1965*

Jimi's band got a gig at the Café Wha?, a downmarket bar in Greenwich Village frequented by aspiring musicians, artists and poets. 'He was playing the Café Wha? for about seven bucks a night...,' remembered Carol Shiroky. 'Always with the gum and his cigarettes, and sticking the cigarette on the top of his guitar.... No, it wasn't an image thing, it was just something that came natural with him – he didn't wanna give up that gum, boy, that was like his wife....' Playing songs such as 'Wild Thing', 'Hey Joe' and Dylan's song, 'Like A Rolling Stone', the Café Wha? gig gave Jimi a chance to experiment and develop his act in front of a broad-minded audience.

The word spread about this wild young guitarist who was using feedback and playing with his teeth. Blues guitarist and singer John Hammond, Jr heard about Jimi, and dropped in to check him out – he was so impressed that he invited Jimi to play with him at his prestigious Café Au Go Go gig. Electric blues guitarist Mike Bloomfield had played on Dylan's *Highway 61 Revisited*, and after he saw Jimi, he was never the same again: 'I didn't even want to pick up a guitar for the next year!' he said.

### LOOK OVER YONDER

Finally, after years of dashed hopes and broken promises, Jimi got the break he had been waiting for. Keith Richards' then-girlfriend, Linda Keith, saw Jimi's potential, and she knew that the Animals' bass player, Chas Chandler, wanted to set up as a manager. Chas was looking for new acts, so she told Chas about Jimi, and persuaded him to take a look.

'This is too good to be true', thought Chas as he watched Jimi perform in the Café Wha?. Surely someone must have signed Jimi already? He was right – Jimi had been signed – several times over! Like many struggling musicians, Jimi would sign anything put in front of him if he thought it would give him a break. Unfortunately, Jimi didn't mention his PPX contract to Chas when he was going around buying up other such contracts for $50 a go....

Chas asked Jimi if he would like to move to London and make records, but Jimi was sceptical. How many times had he heard this routine? 'His only concern was amplifiers...,' Chas later recalled. 'The thing that clinched it was he said, "Do you know Eric Clapton and Jeff Beck?," and as it happened, they were both friends of mine....' Leaving New York as a penniless nobody, Jimi Hendrix would return as a rock star.

# THE JIMI HENDRIX EXPERIENCE

"I HAD THESE DREAMS THAT SOMETHING WAS GONNA HAPPEN,

SEEING THE NUMBER 1966 IN MY SLEEP, SO I WAS JUST PASSING TIME 'TILL THEN.

I WANTED MY OWN SCENE, MAKING MY MUSIC...."

*JIMI HENDRIX*

# PART I

## Are You Experienced?

### 1966–1967

Jimi arrived in London on 24 September 1966 carrying all his worldly possessions in a guitar case – a Fender Stratocaster, some clothes and a jar of face cream. Jimi didn't have a work permit, and the authorities were unwilling to let him into the country. Chas Chandler saved the day and proved his worth as a manager by concocting a story that Jimi was a songwriter returning to collect royalties.

Chas knew many musicians around town, and immediately took Jimi to the house of organ player and band leader Zoot Money, also previously with the Animals, to give Jimi his first taste of the London music scene. A leading R&B outfit, Zoot Money's Big Roll Band had their equipment set up in the basement, so Jimi jammed with Money and his band. That evening Jimi jammed at a London club, where he met an attractive nineteen-year-old, Kathy Etchingham, who instantly became his girlfriend. Two jam sessions and a new girlfriend – not bad for his first day in London!

True to his word, Chas arranged for Jimi to meet Eric Clapton. After leaving John Mayall's Bluesbreakers, Clapton had formed Cream with drummer Ginger Baker and bassist Jack Bruce. Cream were playing at the Polytechnic of Central London on 1 October, and Jimi was invited to jam as long as Clapton stayed onstage. The song chosen was Howlin' Wolf's 'Killing Floor', and as Jimi started to play, Clapton could hardly believe his eyes and ears.

'I'll never forget Eric's face – he just walked off to the side and stood and watched,' recalled Chas. Jimi had a similar effect all on the musicians who saw him jamming in clubs – the Beatles, the Rolling Stones, Pete Townshend, Jeff Beck, etc. All were profoundly impressed by Jimi's musical skills, and some of the guitarists were more than a little intimidated. 'I was sick when I saw him,' confessed Jeff Beck. 'It was like, "What the hell am I going to do tomorrow – get a job at the post office or something?!"'

### Can You See Me?

Jamming with bands around town had introduced Jimi to the music scene, but what he really needed to do now was to put his own band together. A struggling guitarist named Noel Redding had heard about a vacancy with Eric Burdon's New Animals, the re-formation of the previous Animals band. Noel was on the point of quitting the music business altogether and becoming a milkman, but was prepared to give it one last try. Unfortunately, when Noel arrived at the audition, he discovered that the job had already gone. However, Noel was told that Chas was looking for a bass player, so he thought, 'Why not give it a go?'

Jimi jammed with Noel, and each was suitably impressed with the other. Noel immediately saw that Jimi's guitar playing covered all the bases, so it was clear that Jimi wasn't going to need another guitarist. Jimi was taken by Noel's ability to remember the chord changes to songs. Besides, Jimi liked Noel's long, curly hair – that sealed it!

That night Jimi jammed with the Brian Auger Trinity at the Blaises club, where he was spotted by singer Johnny 'the French Elvis' Hallyday, who offered Jimi and his band a short tour of France. With this extra encouragement, Jimi offered Noel the job the next day, and Noel readily accepted. So, now

▲ **The Jimi Hendrix Experience clubbing in Hamburg – from left to right: Mitch, Jimi and Noel.**

*Germany, March 1967*

Jimi had a bass player; all he needed was a drummer – and fast!

Jimi and Chas had already auditioned several drummers, including Aynsley Dunbar, who was playing with John Mayall's Bluesbreakers at the time. Another drummer, John 'Mitch' Mitchell, a former child actor who had worked in the line-up of Georgie Fame and his Blue Flames band, had found himself out of work after Georgie split up his band. Mitch heard about the audition, and squeezed in a jam with Jimi in between a couple of studio sessions. Chas and Jimi couldn't decide – both Aynsley Dunbar and Mitch Mitchell were excellent drummers. In the end, Chas tossed a coin, and fate chose Mitch Mitchell.

All that was needed now was a name for the trio. Since the band was formed around Jimi, it seemed reasonable that his name should be included in the name of the band. 'Jimmy James' from Jimi's New York days had been dropped in favour of the more aggressive and memorable 'Jimmy Hendrix'. But what about a gimmick to grab people's attention? Chas changed 'Jimmy' to 'Jimi', and the final band name then became the 'Jimi Hendrix Experience'. Although nobody at that time had any idea of the impending impact Jimi would have on the rock world, the name appropriately centred

▶ **Feedback!**

*Star Club, Hamburg, Germany, March 1967*

attention on Jimi, and suggested that he was a remarkable phenomenon.

One of the reasons why Chas had moved into band management was that he was sick of being ripped off as a musician in the Animals by double-dealing promoters and unscrupulous managers – they always seemed to make more money than the band did. Ironically, Chas' new business partner was the Animals' old manager, Michael Jeffery – 'well, if you can't beat 'em....' This Michael Jeffery was a curious character – a hard-headed, tough businessman who liked to drop acid and who had worked undercover in the Intelligence Corps. Mysterious and evasive, Jeffery was also a shrewd negotiator, and for this trait Chas was glad to have him on his side. The set-up was that Chas would take care of the musical side of things, and Michael would take care of the business side.

Chas and Michael initially saw the Jimi Hendrix Experience as essentially Jimi, plus two musicians who were employed to back him. Consequently, only Jimi was given a management contract, but all three were offered a production contract that gave each of them a share of 2.5 per cent of record sales royalties, with Chas and Michael receiving 20 per cent. Not a particularly good deal for the band, but Jimi had never been business-minded, and no-one knew whether the band would take off or not. The production contract that all three signed didn't differentiate between the status of the individual members, and Noel and Mitch thought little of it at the time. However, when sales of Hendrix recordings began to rise dramatically in the 80s, the lack of remuneration received by Noel and Mitch became an extremely contentious and bitter issue.

Once they had organized the business side of things, the Jimi Hendrix Experience went into rehearsals for their French tour supporting Johnny Hallyday. Money was going to be tight at first, so Chas asked Michael for some cash to help get the band on the road. Living up to his mysterious and evasive reputation, Michael's funds seemed to be tied up elsewhere, and Chas had to sell some of his bass guitars to keep the band going – although Jeffery's secretary, Trixie Sullivan, later claimed this was 'a load of crap', as apparently, 'he [Chas] never did' [sell the guitars].

On 12 October 1966, the Jimi Hendrix Experience flew to France for their four-date tour. With other bands on the bill, the Experience were scheduled to play for only fifteen minutes. Their set included cover versions of 'Killing Floor', 'Hey Joe' and 'Wild Thing', since at this early stage the band did not yet have any original material.

Already working on stage presentation, Jimi stood in the wings of the Olympia theatre in Paris while he was being introduced, and played a couple of short bursts of guitar before he strolled on stage – a simple idea, but the audience lapped it up.

On this first occasion of the band playing publicly together, Mitch got a shock – he hadn't seen Jimi in action before a live audience, and he was completely amazed by the dramatic change in Jimi's persona. 'He was a quiet bloke, at least until he got on stage. It was on the first gig that we saw the whole other person, completely different from anything I'd seen before, even during rehearsals.' Fired up by the audience, quiet and mild-mannered Jimi

▼ **Unpublished shot from a photo session for the cover of the first LP *Are You Experienced?***

*London, early 1967*

▲ **Jimi takes a relaxing cigarette break in his flat.**

*London, early 1967*

would be transformed into an extrovert showman, playing the guitar behind his head and with his teeth – much to the audience's delight.

Returning to Britain at the end of their tour, the band discovered that the tour had done little to help their finances, which were in dire straits. Mitch and Noel had to play sessions to make ends meet, and Jimi borrowed £50 from his former employer, Little Richard, who was in London doing a gig at the time.

### HEY JOE

With the band's need for cash and greater exposure, their next obvious move was to record a single. Chas wanted Jimi to record his version of 'Hey Joe,' a song originally written by an obscure American West Coast folk singer/songwriter, Billy Roberts, that had been an earlier hit for an LA band called the Leaves, and had also been recorded by many other artists. Said Jimi of 'Hey Joe', one of his signature tunes: 'Lots of people have done different arrangements of it, and Timmy Rose was the first to do it slowly – I like it played slowly.' Although Jimi wanted his version of Howlin' Wolf's 'Killing Floor' or the standard 'Land of 1000 Dances' on the flip side, Chas objected, for since the Beatles had started writing their own songs, any new artist wanting to be taken seriously had to be able to show he could write original material. Chas told Jimi to write something of his own, and Jimi came up with 'Stone Free' – the first of several memorable songs Jimi was to write.

Back in the studio to start their recording, Jimi plugged into his Marshall amp, set the controls on ten and started playing. 'Turn it down, man – it's too fuckin' loud!' screamed Chas, barely able to make himself heard above Jimi's guitar. A straight-talking Geordie, Chas may have been in awe of Jimi's talent, but he wasn't afraid to stand up to Jimi when necessary. It wasn't the first time Jimi had heard this, either; throughout his previous career as a sideman, Jimi had often taken flak for playing too loud, but he thought that surely now that he had his own band, he could play as loud as he liked. However, Chas objected to Jimi's volume level in the studio for the simple reason that the equipment just wasn't designed to cope with it. Reluctantly, Jimi turned the volume controls down.

▼ **The Experience were very popular in many countries of continental Europe, such as Germany.**
*Big Apple, München, Germany, November 1966*

◀ **A great shot of Jimi in full concert flight.**

*Star Club, Hamburg, March 1967*

Like many of the Beatles' early singles such as 'A Hard Day's Night' and 'Help!', 'Hey Joe' has an instantly recognisable intro – Jimi plays unison 'E' notes on the top two strings, eliciting a 'chiming' sound. However, for the clubgoers who had seen Hendrix in action, the recorded 'Hey Joe' was something of a disappointment. Although 'Hey Joe' contained a wonderful intro and an exquisitely phrased guitar solo, the emphasis was on the song rather than on Jimi's guitar-playing antics that were so successful in reaching a larger audience. Chas took the demo to Decca, the record company best-known for turning down the Beatles. True to form, they also turned down the Jimi Hendrix Experience!

Things were getting desperate as funds began to run low. Jimi was jamming with the VIPs at the Scotch of St James club when he was spotted by the Who's management team of Chris Stamp and Kit Lambert. Said Chris Stamp: 'This guy was something special that we wanted to get involved with... so when we checked it out, we found out he had a manager, so we couldn't manage him, we couldn't produce him, so the only thing left was the record deal'. Conveniently, Stamp and Lambert were starting up their own record label, Track Records. 'He [Jimi] was our first signing... apart from the Who. "Hey Joe" came out on Polydor because the labels of Track Records weren't finished.... The deal really hinged on what we guaranteed to do with Jimi, I mean we guaranteed "Ready, Steady, Go!"'

Released on 16 December 1966, 'Hey Joe' b/w 'Stone Free' met with good reviews from the music press and entered the UK single charts at number thirty-eight, quickly moving into the top ten, where it peaked at number four. The Experience played live on the British TV shows 'Ready, Steady, Go!' and 'Top Of The Pops', and pretty soon they were receiving constant media attention and playing a steady stream of club gigs. Meanwhile, Michael Jeffery disappeared to the States, coming back with an extremely good record deal from Warner Bros. All in all, things were beginning to look good for the Jimi Hendrix Experience.

▼ **Various 1967 material from 'The Jimi Hendrix Experience Official Fan Club of Great Britain'. The club ran out of money and was disbanded in mid 1969.**

### SMASHING TIMES

In November, the band packed their bags and set off to play four dates at the Big Apple club in Munich, Germany with their new roadie, Gerry Stickells. For the first time, Jimi intentionally smashed a guitar, although admittedly he hadn't set out to. Grabbed by enthusiastic fans, Jimi had ended up in the audience. He threw his guitar back onstage, but the impact broke some of the strings and cracked the guitar's body. Following the maxim, 'If you make a mistake, do it again and they'll think you meant it,' Jimi pounced on his guitar and smashed it to pieces. The audience loved it – this wild act of destruction – and it became an occasional part of Jimi's act, as well as adding the theme of destruction to the iconography of rock 'n' roll.

▲ Single, 'Purple Haze', Polydor, Germany, 1967.

▲ Single, 'Purple Haze', Track, England, 1967.

After Munich, The Experience returned to the studio to work on 'Purple Haze,' their second single and first for Track Records' new label. Lyrically, the song was inspired by a science fiction book called *Night Of Light* by Philip José Farmer – Jimi loved science fiction, and would incorporate its futuristic ideas into some of his later songs. Like 'Hey Joe', 'Purple Haze' had an immediately recognizable intro, with the guitar and bass playing notes forming the diminished fifth interval. Known as the 'Diablo in Musica' by the Spanish Inquisition, this interval was thought to summon the forces of darkness – the musical equivalent of knocking on Satan's front door. The main riff uses the raunchy, 'crunching' sound of the '7#9' chord, which has since become known to guitarists as the 'Hendrix chord'. By no means the first to use this chord, it was Jimi who made it a permanent fixture in the rock guitarist's chord book.

Jimi also started using effects pedals – a Fuzz Face to further distort the sound, and an Octavia, a custom-built device designed for Jimi by electronics boffin Roger Mayer, which added a note an octave higher than the one played. As Jimi later commented, ' "Purple Haze" was one step on the way to getting our own personal sound.' Again, they had a success on their hands, as 'Purple Haze' quickly peaked at number three in the UK charts.

The Jimi Hendrix Experience were now set to play their first UK tour. As the tour was booked before their recent success, the Experience found themselves playing on the same bill as Engelbert Humperdinck, Cat Stevens and the Walker Brothers – a rather unusual line-up, to say the least. Package tours were commonplace at the time, and were a good way to break new artists, although whether or not an Engelbert Humperdinck fan would be receptive to the Jimi Hendrix Experience was another matter! Backstage at London's Astoria for the tour's first date on 31 March, Chas and the band racked their brains for a publicity stunt to grab the headlines. Smashing a guitar was out of the question – too obvious!

'It's a pity you can't set fire to your guitar,' ventured journalist Keith Altham. 'A solid body would never burn.' Quicker than you could say 'fire hazard', Chas dispatched roadie Gerry Stickells to buy some lighter fluid.

JIMI HENDRIX EXPERIENCE

HEY JOE-STC

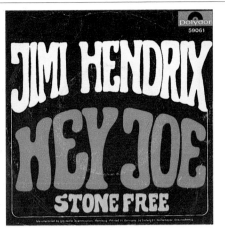

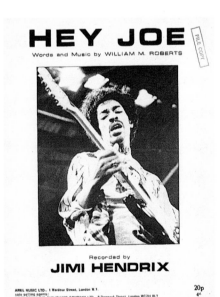

1. Single, Polydor, Germany, 1966.
2. CD single, Barclay, France, 1967.
3. Typical advertisement for 'Hey Joe' in the English music press, January 1967.
4. Single, Polydor, England, 1966.
5. Single, Polydor, Italy, 1975.
6. Single, Barclay.
7. Single, Polydor, Japan, 1967.
8. Sheet music for 20 pence — those were the days!

▲ Single, Polydor, Japan, 1968.

▶ Advertisement in the English music
magazines.

*March 1967*

◀ Advertisement, USA, 1967. Since Reprise
representatives hadn't seen Jimi Hendrix
perform at that point in time, they didn't have
a clue on how to promote 'Hey Joe' – perhaps
they thought they had signed a cousin of
James Brown or Otis Redding?

▲ ▼ ▶ **Various biographical material produced in England during the early JHE period in 1967.**

During the last song, appropriately called 'Fire', Jimi whipped out the fluid canister and squirted it onto the guitar. Straddling the instrument, Jimi struck a match. But the guitar wouldn't light! Jimi persevered, collecting a little pile of used matches, then eventually – whoosh! – the guitar caught fire. Just for good measure, Jimi swung the guitar around his head a few times. The security officer was apoplectic, but the deed was done and the publicity gained Jimi some useful notoriety.

The Experience's third single, 'The Wind Cries Mary', showed the gentler side of Jimi's music and was written after Jimi had a domestic row with his girlfriend Kathy (Mary is her middle name). By now the band and Chas were comfortable working together in the studio, and according to Chas, 'The Wind Cries Mary' was recorded in only twenty minutes. It was their third single – and their third hit.

Jimi's confidence noticeably grew in his stage manner and his singing as the Experience played more and more gigs. However, live shows were rarely smooth-running affairs, mainly due to the primitive state of musical equipment technology. Jimi liked the distortion and sustain from a cranked amplifier, and for cleaner, quieter sounds he would ease back the volume control on his guitar. He would often joke with the audience: 'Plug your ears! Watch out for your ears!' Not surprisingly, Jimi's penchant for playing with everything on 'ten' (aka 'The Hendrix setting') would take its toll on

▲ **All dressed up for the party at the Variety Club of
Great Britain's 'Tribute to the Recording Industry'
luncheon.**

*Dorchester Hotel, London, 9 May 1967*

**THE WIND CRIES MARY**
Words & Music by JIMI HENDRIX

THE — JIMI — HENDRIX — EXPERIENCE

Recorded on TRACK Records

A. SCHROEDER MUSIC PUBLISHING CO. LTD., (YAMETA) 3/-
15. BERKELEY STREET. LONDON. W.1.
sole selling agents:– CAMPBELL, CONNELLY & CO., LTD., 10, Denmark Street, London, W. C. 2.

**7**

1. Single, Track, England, 1967.
2. Single, Polydor, Germany, 1967.
3. Single, Barclay, France, 1967.
4. Promotional poster, Track, England, 1967.
5. Review from *Disc and Music Echo* (England), 29 April 1967.
6. Single, Polydor, Japan, 1967.
7. Sheet music, England, 1967.
8. Single, Barclay, France, 1967.
9. Single, Barclay, France.

**8**

**9**

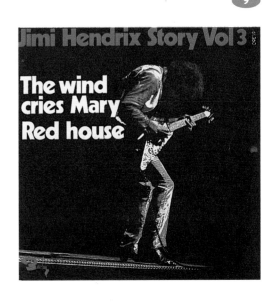

the amplifiers, and would also make it difficult for the Experience to hear one another. As Mitch later commented: 'Drummers, of course, weren't miked up at all – there was no PA as such, just whatever came with the venue, no back line, no monitors. I could barely hear anything at all, you really had to rely on watching people's hands move and hope you were playing in the same time; very difficult. You couldn't hear any vocals and half the time neither could the audience. We did get vocal monitors for front stage, but nothing for the fold back, certainly nothing for me.'

Also, Jimi's vigorous use of the vibrato arm of his Strat often put the guitar out of tune, which sometimes meant tuning up after every single song. Jimi would chat or joke with the audience as he retuned, but he was a perfectionist and the technical difficulties experienced when playing live often frustrated him.

The Experience would never play a song the same way twice, and thus had more in common with jazz musicians than some of the rock bands of the time who would perform almost verbatim versions of their records. As Jimi explained, 'You're not actually tryin' to get that same sound because that's been had on a record. You can leave the concert and go home and play the record if you want to hear it just like that. We give you another side of it.' This attitude to performance made live gigs more exciting for the audience, as they never knew exactly what was going to happen.

The release of the Jimi Hendrix Experience's debut album *Are You Experienced?* in Britain on 12 May 1967 met with rave reviews, and the

1. LP, Track, England.
2. LP, Polydor, Germany.
3. LP, First Record, Taiwan.
4. LP, Reprise, USA, 1967.

album eventually reached number three in the charts. Keith Altham, reviewing the album for the *New Musical Express*, wrote: 'Hendrix is a new dimension in electrical guitar music, launching what amounts to a one-man assault upon the nerve cells. The LP is a brave effort by Hendrix to produce a musical form which is original and exciting.'

Altham hit the nail on the head. Jimi Hendrix practically invented the electric guitar, showing its myriad boundless possibilities. An article in *Guitar Player* magazine written by Andy Ellis almost thirty years after the release of *Are You Experienced?* stated that 'the story of the electric guitar will forever

2

3

4

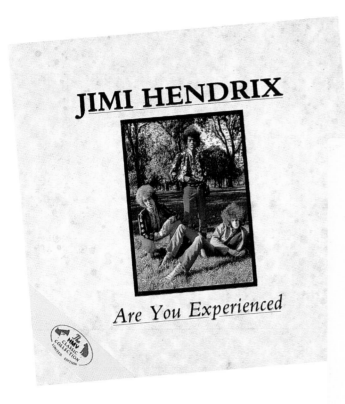

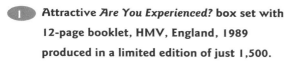

No. CD1173

1. Attractive *Are You Experienced?* box set with 12-page booklet, HMV, England, 1989 produced in a limited edition of just 1,500.

2. Reel box. *Are You Experienced?* Reprise.

3. Reel-to-reel, Bell & Howell, USA, 1967.

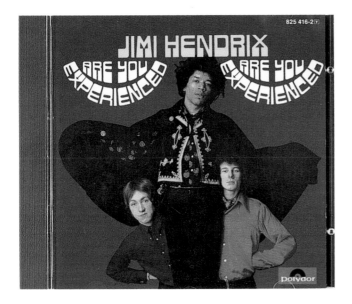

4 CD, Polydor, Germany.

5 CD, Reprise, USA.

6 LP, Barclay, France – re-release.

7 LP, Rotation/Polydor, Germany – re-release.

8 LP, Barclay, France, 1967 – original release.

▲ Single, Barclay, France, 1968.

◄ Single, Polydor, Japan, 1968.

▲ Rare clothes hanger from 1967
(England).

be told in two parts: Before Jimi and After Jimi'. Other guitarists, such as Jeff Beck and Pete Townshend, had experimented with feedback, but neither had harnessed it to the same musical effect that Jimi did at the beginning of 'Foxy Lady,' the album's opening track. But it wasn't all 'screamin 'n' wailin' guitars. 'May This Be Love', like the earlier 'The Wind Cries Mary', showed the sensitive side to Jimi's music, and also showed one of Jimi's early uses of sound to paint pictures – the song began with Jimi's descending slide down the fretboard, evoking the waterfall named in the song's original title. 'Red House' reminded listeners of Jimi's blues roots, Jimi beginning the song with a common chord shape that can be traced right back to bluesman Robert Johnson. 'I Don't Live Today' began with an ominous drum beat from Mitch that sounded like a native American drum pattern – Jimi was one-sixteenth Cherokee Indian, and in concert he often dedicated the song to the American Indian.

The writing of the song 'Manic Depression' showed how Jimi could be inspired at the drop of a hat. Depressed after a guitar was stolen and having to endure yet another press reception, Jimi had a conversation with Chas, who told him he sounded like a manic depressive. Sparked off by this comment, Jimi went off to the reception, and as he was answering questions, he was meanwhile writing a song in his head about manic depression! Played in waltz time, but with a triplet feel, 'Manic Depression' sounds as if Johann 'King of the Waltz' Strauss had rolled a great big fat joint, slung a Strat over his shoulder and cranked his amp up to eleven!

In 'Third Stone From The Sun', Jimi used octaves in the style of jazz guitarist Wes Montgomery, and pushed the tonal possibilities of the electric guitar even further, using feedback and extreme vibrato arm abuse to create a sonic picture of interstellar travel. For the guitar solo in the song 'Are You Experienced?' Jimi recorded his guitar normally then reversed the tape for a 'backwards' guitar solo – not only was Jimi experimenting with the guitar, he was also experimenting with the recording studio equipment, something he would explore further on his next two albums.

Are you experienced? Britain certainly was. America had better – Jimi Hendrix was returning with a vengeance.

▲ **Jimi easily blended in with the crowd, as seen in front of his flat at 34 Montagu Square, London W1.**
*February 1967*

▼ **(Right and left) Jimi's idea of home-cooking....**
*London, January 1967*

# PART 2

## AXIS: BOLD AS LOVE

▶ **Jimi soaking up the Monterey vibes.**
*18 June 1967*

Dressed in a yellow ruffled shirt, tight red pants, an embroidered waistcoat and a psychedelic jacket topped off with a pink feather boa, Jimi took the stage at the Monterey Pop Festival on 18 June 1967.

Jimi checked his sound with a short burst of rhythm guitar, then immediately tore into the intro of 'Killing Floor', sounding like three guitarists playing at the same time – an exuberant exorcism of all the frustration he had experienced in America during his years of struggle. With Mitch and Noel supporting him every inch of the way, this was going to be one show the audience would never forget.

Earlier that day, Jimi had had a backstage war of words with Pete Townshend of the Who. Both bands used destruction as part of their stage act, and each was afraid of being upstaged by the other. Unable to agree about who would go on first, the bands asked John Phillips from the Mamas and the Papas, who was part of the festival's organization, to toss a coin – the second time the toss of a coin would play an important part in Jimi's career! Jimi lost and had to go on after the Who, so he vowed that when he got onstage he would 'pull out all the stops.'

The Who ended their set by trashing their equipment, leaving the audience stunned – if this was the 'summer of love,' someone had forgotten to tell Pete Townshend & Co. The audience got their heads back together by mellowing out to the sounds of the Grateful Dead while Jimi psyched himself up backstage. 'I'm looking forward to tonight, man,' Jimi had told Eric Burdon earlier that afternoon. 'The spaceship's really gonna take off tonight.'

'I'd like to introduce you to a very good friend, a fellow countryman of yours,' announced Brian Jones from the Rolling Stones. 'A brilliant performer, the most exciting guitarist I've ever heard. The Jimi Hendrix Experience!' Jimi used every trick in the book of cool stage moves to impress the audience, and then added a few new ones. Playing the guitar with one hand, plucking the strings with his teeth... the audience had never anything quite like this before! But it wasn't all flash – Jimi endeared to the audience with a version of Bob Dylan's 'Like A Rolling Stone', showing he was just as hip to new sounds as they were. Jimi added take on the blues, drastically reworking B.B. King's slow blues song Me, Baby' into an up-tempo romp. But Jimi the performer also k

◀ **'International Monterey Pop Festival'.**
*18 June 1967*

and screaming in protest. Retreating to his amps, Jimi returned with a can of lighter fluid, and ejaculated flammable liquid all over the guitar. Lighting the guitar with a match, Jimi straddled his instrument and, like a pyromaniacal shaman, encouraged it to burn. Picking the guitar up, he swings it around his head and brings it crashing to the stage floor, breaking the neck and then throwing parts of the decimated guitar into the audience.

'Ladies and gentlemen – Jimi Hendrix!' Some of the audience applauded wildly, others just stood stock-still, unable to take in what they had just seen. Backstage, Jimi's fellow artists rushed over to congratulate him. Jimi's Monterey performance established him in America almost overnight, and two days later the group got a taste of just how popular they had instantly become. Promoter Bill Graham had booked the Experience to play for six nights supporting the Jefferson Airplane at the Fillmore West in California, but as Chas recalled, 'Hendrix murdered the Jefferson Airplane. After one night they gave top of the bill to Jimi.'

1

2

3

4

5

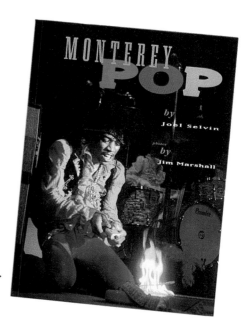

6

1  Video, Virgin, England, 1987.

2  LP, Atlantic, France, 1970.

3  This box release comes with a Monterey
   T-shirt, but actually contains the CDs
   *Radio One* and *The Jimi Hendrix Concerts*
   – Castle Communications, England, 1991.

4  This special box released by Rhino (USA
   1992) contains four CDs (which includes
   the JHE set from Monterey) and a book
   on Monterey.

5  LP, Reprise, USA, 1970.

6  One of many publications on the Monterey Pop Festival
   – Chronicle Books, USA, 1992.

▲ **Jimi used a Gibson 'Flying V' mainly for his blues songs.**

*'Olympia', Paris, France, 9 October 1967*

THEY MADE
THIS ONE
WITHOUT MY
KNOWLEDGE

JIMI HENDRIX
and THAT record.

# Pop man Jimi to sue a disc firm

NOT for nothing is Jimi Hendrix called The Wild Man of Pop.

He has a way-out hair-style, a raving stage act . . . and now a hit-size grievance against a giant British disc firm.

In fact, he is to sue the company—Decca Records.

The fuss is revolving around a record called "Hush Now," which Decca have recently issued on their London label.

The record, says the 22-year-old coloured guitarist and leader of the Jimi Hendrix Experience, was put out without his consent.

### By PETER OAKES

He is claiming High Court damages against Decca.

Jimi, who has had four hit records since coming to Britain a year ago, said: "I walked into a record store and saw this record of mine.

"When I played it I discovered that it had been recorded with a jam session I did in New York.

"We had only been practising in the studio. I had no idea it was being recorded."

#### Independent

Jimi went on: "On one side of the disc in 'Hush Now' I only play the guitar. The singer's voice has been super-imposed.

"On the other, 'Flashing,' all I do is play a couple of notes.

"Man, I was shocked when I heard it!"

Jimi — his record called "Purple Haze" reached No. 3 in the charts earlier this year—

is being represented by solicit David Jacobs.

His previous hits have be issued by Polydor, an indep dent label.

So far the disc in dispute made little impact on record-buying public.

On the record, credit both the numbers are gi Jimi Hendrix and Knight, who is an American soul singer.

A spokesman for Decca said: "We recently released a single recording of Jimi Hendrix made in America, over which there is some dispute.

"We acquired the material from an American producer who said it had been recorded in New York.

"We cannot make any further comment as the matter is in the hands of our solicitors."

Five months ago Jimi was reported to have been banned by the Daughters of the American Revolution, the American women's organisation.

They felt he was too erotic for his audiences of predominantly seven to 12-year-olds.

# JIMI HENDRIX QUITS MONKEE TOUR

### 'Think Mickey Mouse has replaced me'

JIMI HENDRIX phoned the NME on Saturday with the sensational news that he had quit the Monkees' American tour after only seven shows. The Hendrix Experience will remain in the U.S. for at least two more weeks to complete their new single and undertake some further bookings on the West Coast.

"Firstly they gave us the 'death' spot on the show—right before the Monkees were due on," Jimi declared. "The audience just screamed and yelled for the Monkees! Finally, they agreed to let us go on first and things were much better. We got screams and good reaction, and some kids even rushed the stage.

"But we were not getting any billing—all the posters for the show just screamed out—MONKEES!

"Then some parents who brought their young kids complained that our act was vulgar. We decided it was just the wrong audience. I think they're replacing me with Mickey Mouse!

"There was no tension between us and the Monkees whatever. And all the rumours about being segregated on the plane were just nonsense. I got on well with both Micky and Peter and we fooled around a lot together.

"There was a fantastic girl singer on the tour—an Australian girl called Lynne Randell. She's got a record out in Britain, so you may be hearing more of her.

"In New York we all went out to see the Electric Circus club in the Village, which just completely blew my mind. There was a group called the Seeds playing there but they had all these funny little acts going on between things. One guy walked up on to the stage and stood

there and growled for about five minutes, then he said 'Thank you,' and walked off! There was another guy who came on in a strait-jacket and just rolled around on the floor for half-an-hour. Then some funny little guys came swinging down on ropes from the ceiling. We couldn't believe it!

"I've been reading those reports about my new single being 'The Burning Of The Midnight Lamp'. Well it's true that I have recorded a track with those words in the song but I'm not sure that that is going

JIMI HENDRIX wears the expression he might put on if you mention Monkee audiences in America to him!

to be either the title or the single. We had a great time in LA, where Dave Crosby and a group called the Electric Flag came round to see us at the Whisky A Go Go. I love the West Coast, all those beautiful people.

"Chas (Chandler) and Mike (Jeffries) are making arrangements for an autumn tour of Britain for us when we get back—it would be great if we get some of these really groovy American groups from the West Coast on the show with us," Jimi concluded.

 Left: *People* (England), 17 December 1967; right: *New Musical Express* (England) 29 July 1967.

The LA rock scene welcomed the Experience with open arms. Peter Tork from the Monkees invited Jimi to stay with him at his Laurel Canyon estate, where Jimi met Joni Mitchell, Judy Collins, David Crosby and Mike Bloomfield. Jimi was also introduced to Devon Wilson, a hip and attractive black 'super-groupie' who would later become his girlfriend. Leaving LA, the Experience flew to New York, and Jimi took advantage of some rare spare time to see Frank Zappa and the Mothers of Invention at the Garrick Theatre in Greenwich Village, joining them onstage for a jam.

New York's Scene Club was a popular hangout for musicians, and Jimi would jam there at any opportunity. However, musical thrills were not the only kicks to be had in the Scene, as Mitch recalled. 'It was the first place we

really encountered groupies on a mass scale. Hendrix used to call them "Band-Aids". I've been asked many times if the debauchery didn't become boring. The answer is no – most entertaining. In America they seemed a lot more organized – shall I say professional. There was definitely a pecking order there, almost a union.'

Behind the scenes, Michael Jeffery had been working on a tour. 'I've just done it, a great deal, a nationwide tour,' Michael told Chas over the phone, sounding pleased with himself. Michael had arranged a tour with the Monkees, and Chas couldn't believe his ears. 'Are you out of your fucking mind?' he asked. The Monkees were a squeaky-clean pop group, manufactured by American TV producers to star in a TV series inspired by the Beatles' film *A Hard Day's Night*. It was difficult to imagine a more unsuitable combination than the Experience and the Monkees, but the Monkees themselves were keen on the idea – it might give them a little more 'hip' credibility – and Michael thought it would get Jimi extra publicity, since in America the Monkees were almost as popular as the Beatles.

Not surprisingly, the bizarre combination did not work. After all, the very young audience were there to see the Monkees, and had little interest in these three freaky guys with long hair who played too loud. Jimi had an artistic temperament, and if things were going badly he made little effort to hide it. He would skip lines in songs or play songs too fast just to get them over with, both of which annoyed Noel Redding, who thought such behaviour was unprofessional and inexcusable. 'They gave us the death spot on the show, right before the Monkees were due on,' complained Jimi. 'The audience just screamed and yelled for the Monkees.' The Experience soldiered on, but after seven dates they could take no more.

Chas had suspected the worst from the very beginning, and had made emergency arrangements with promoter Dick Clark for the band to bail out. A story was needed for the press, so a tale was spun whereby the Daughters of the American Revolution, a hyper-conservative US organization, had insisted Jimi be taken off the tour to avoid further offending Monkees' fans.

Back in New York, Jimi visited some of his old haunts and caught up with old friends. Jimi's ex-girlfriend Fay Pridgeon could hardly believe how far he had come in only a few months – the struggling guitarist who had been forced to beg to jam with club bands was now a rock star on first-name terms with the Beatles and Rolling Stones. Jimi's financial position had also improved, and he made a point of repaying old debts. Jimi had once borrowed forty dollars from a friend, and when he found him, he handed him a bundle of hundred- and thousand-dollar bills, saying, 'Here man – take what you need.' Jimi renewed his friendship with John Hammond, Jr, and they jammed together. Hammond recalls that on a couple of nights Eric Clapton was also in town, so the three of them all jammed together.

Jimi also met up with Curtis Knight and Ed Chalpin. Jimi and Chalpin went out for dinner together and Chalpin seemed to be in a pretty good mood considering that Jimi had broken his contract with him. 'No hard feelings?' wondered Jimi, believing that things had since smoothed over. However, he couldn't have been more wrong, as he was soon to discover!

1  Single, Track, England, 1967.

2  Single, Polydor, Germany, 1967.

3  Sheet music published in England, 1967.

4  Single, Barclay, France, 1967.

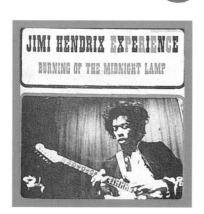

## I'M GONNA WAVE MY FREAK FLAG HIGH...

Chalpin announced suddenly that he was going to sue. He had already started by issuing writs against Polydor and Track in the UK to stop Jimi recording for them, and was going to issue a writ against Warner Bros. in the USA. Chalpin's company PPX had an exclusive hold over Jimi until October 1968, and he was going to take full advantage of it.

Yet despite Chalpin's instigation of legal action, Jimi agreed to go into PPX's Studio 76 in New York to do some recording with Curtis Knight. Chalpin was producing the session, and he reassured Jimi that his name wouldn't be used on the recordings. Jimi was either too trusting or too naive, as Chalpin was lying. Jimi Hendrix records were going to mean big bucks, and there was no way Chalpin would pass up on this golden opportunity to cash in. In the forthcoming years, these sessions would form the basis of countless Curtis Knight albums, all produced with the intention of cashing in on Jimi's name, and Chalpin would make a handsome $1 million out of Jimi. Jimi claimed that he had done the sessions as a favour to his old friend Curtis Knight on the condition that his name wasn't used if the recordings were released, and that Knight had agreed.

The battle of the writs commenced. Chalpin was involved with Capitol in America, their sister company in the UK being Decca. Decca now wanted to release a Curtis Knight single recorded with Jimi called 'How Would You

▲ **Broomstick blues during a photocall at the 7¹/₂ Club, London W1.**
*9 January 1967*

Feel?' ahead of the next Jimi Hendrix Experience single, but after Track and Polydor threatened counter-litigation, Decca got cold feet. The single was quickly withdrawn, then Track released the very same song just one week later!

The next Experience single, 'The Burning Of The Midnight Lamp', featured a Wah-wah pedal, which Jimi quickly added to his ever-expanding repertoire of sounds. With his keen ear for the overall arrangement of a song, Jimi picked out the song's opening melody on electric harpsichord – later he would embellish 'Little Wing' from the second Experience album, *Axis: Bold As Love*, with glockenspiel. With a poignant introduction and an introspective lyric, 'Midnight Lamp' was the first Jimi Hendrix Experience song to fail to reach the top ten, although Jimi wasn't worried – 'That song was the song I liked best of all we did. I'm glad it didn't make it big and get thrown around.'

Meanwhile, the *Are You Experienced?* LP was released in America with a different track listing – Jimi's first three UK singles were included, and three of the original tracks dropped, including 'Red House' – much to Jimi's disgust. 'Everybody was scared to release it in America! They said, "Man, America don't like blues, man!" Blues is a part of America.'

During the autumn of 1967, the Experience concentrated their efforts on the eagerly awaited follow-up to *Are You Experienced?* in Olympic Sound Studios in Barnes, London. As with *Are You Experienced?*, Chas was in

▲ **Many of the early Jimi Hendrix Experience recordings were laid down at De Lane Lea Music Ltd. studio in London WC2. Here's a picture of Jimi and Noel working things out.**

*23 October 1967*

▶ **Poster published by Dutch magazine *Hitweek* in late 1967.**

as producer, but now Jimi was less reticent in the studio and wanted a much bigger say in how things should sound, with the help of engineer Eddie Kramer, who had been involved in a few of the band's earlier recordings. Roadie Neville Chesters observed: 'Everybody who ever was around Jimi looked to him. When he was working you didn't question what he was doing. I remember a couple of times during *Axis* Chas was sort of questioning things. And Jimi would go along with it. Chas would say, "I think you ought to do it like that" and Jimi would say, "Yeah, yeah" and then he would do it how he wanted it anyway!'

Recording and mixing completed, the Experience could relax a little. Jimi took the master tapes to a party, keen to let people hear the new record.

Published by Hitweek, Alexander Boersstraat 30, Amsterdam © 1967
Design by Theo van den Boogaard

Jimi **HENDRIX** Experience

HAROLD DAVISON and TITO BURN present

illustration/design A Litri/Paul Martin & Associates

# THE PINK FLOYD

**THE NICE**     **THE EIRE APPA**
**THE OUTER LIMITS** Compere **PETE DRUM**

# The MOVE

# THE AMEN CORNER

Later, Jimi returned home, but without one of the tapes – he had managed to lose the master tape for side A! With the deadline for the delivery of the master tapes imminent, there was no other option – they had to go back into the studio to remix the first side of the record in a marathon eleven-hour session.

The Experience's second UK tour began on 14 November, although this time they were headlining, with a grand total of six support acts, including the Move and Pink Floyd. On 27 November in Belfast, Jimi was told of a fan in hospital who couldn't attend the concert after suffering an asthma attack – Jimi spoke to the fan on the telephone and sent him a souvenir. This day was Jimi's twenty-fifth birthday, and backstage he was presented with a birthday cake.

The band were on the road when *Axis: Bold As Love* was released on 1 December 1967. The album met with enthusiastic reviews. *Melody Maker*'s reviewer could barely contain himself: 'It's all too much. Amaze your ears, boggle

JIMI HENDRIX cover, said to cost £3,000. This is just the top half of a magnificent coloured painting.

▲ Review for *Axis: Bold As Love* LP in *New Musical Express* (England), 25 November 1967.

◄ Programme for the November/December 1967 package tour.

1. LP, Track, England, 1967.
2. LP, Barclay, France, 1968 – original release of *Axis: Bold As Love*.
3. MC, Reprise, USA, 1968.
4. CD, *Axis: Bold As Love*, Polydor, Germany. Also available in the UK.
5. LP, Karussell, Germany – re-release of *Axis: Bold As Love*.
6. LP, Barclay, France, re-release of *Axis: Bold As Love*.

▼ Expensive box set containing a photobook, CD, and a
'Certificate of Authentication' – UFO, England, 1991.

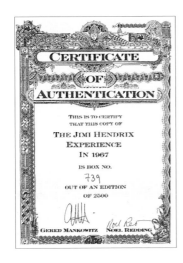

▲ Single, Polydor, Germany, 1968.

◀ Single, Barclay, France, 1968.

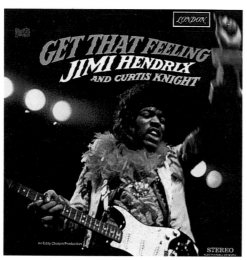

▲ LP, London Records, Holland, 1967.

your mind, flip your lid, do what you want, but please get into Hendrix like you never have before – it's just too much.'

*Axis: Bold As Love* further explored the sensitive and reflective side of Jimi Hendrix. 'To people who are not listening very much,' Jimi commented, *Axis: Bold As Love* 'will put them to sleep right away.' Continuing a thread started by 'May This Be Love' on the debut album and that would run on to the Experience's third album, songs such as 'Little Wing,' 'Castles Made Of Sand' and 'One Rainy Wish' featured a highly evocative chord/melody style of guitar playing. By combining chord fragments with melodies, Jimi blurred the traditional distinction between 'lead' guitar and 'rhythm' guitar. Jimi had picked up parts of this technique from Curtis Mayfield, but had taken it much further. When playing this style, Jimi would often use his right-hand thumb to hold down notes on the fretboard, helped by his unusually long fingers. Said Mitch: 'One thing that struck me about Jimi early on was his hands. He had these huge hands, his thumbs were nearly as long as his fingers.'

Jimi again used the Wah-wah pedal in the jazzy 'Up From The Skies', with Mitch getting into the spirit of the track by playing with brushes instead of drum sticks, apparently a suggestion from Noel. Mitch would often create drums parts which perfectly fitted and complemented Jimi's music. As Eddie Kramer recalled, 'Mitch had the ability to almost read what Jimi was thinking. Jimi would never cease to be amazed at Mitch's ability to play ridiculous things.'

Lyrically, 'If Six Was Nine' was a bold assertion of Jimi's individuality, Jimi getting his own back for every time someone had stared at him for his 'freaky' clothes. 'White collar conservative flashin' down the street pointin' their plastic finger at me... but I'm gonna wave my freak flag high.' Typically for Jimi, there was no malice intended in the lyrics. 'I don't say nothin' bad about nobody. It just says, man, let them go on and screw up theirs, just as long as they don't mess with me.'

The first and final tracks of *Axis: Bold As Love* saw Jimi exploiting the technology of the recording studio. 'EXP' opens the album, and features Mitch and Jimi in a mock interview about 'space ships and even space people,' a vari-speed device being used to speed up interviewer Mitch's voice to a breathless, over-excited squeal and to slow down Jimi's voice to an other-worldly, omniscient drawl. The interview ends with spaceman Jimi setting off in his space ship, represented by a cacophony of electric guitar and amplifier abuse.

For the album's closing track, 'Bold As Love,' Jimi stretched the creative talents of his recording team, Eddie Kramer and fellow engineer George Chkiantz treating the end of the track with stereo phasing. 'That's the sound I've been hearing in my dreams!' gushed Jimi, delighted that he was beginning to unlock some of the sounds in his head.

Jimi was less happy with Chalpin's December 1967 release of a Curtis Knight album, *Get That Feeling*, which was intended to exploit Jimi's involvement – 'Get That Cash' would have been a more appropriate title. But the year ended on a high note with a great Experience concert at the Olympia in London on 22 December, supported by the Who and Pink Floyd, amongst others. Jimi had good reason to be happy – he had established himself as a major recording artist, and finally felt that he was in control of his own destiny. Little was he aware that, from now on, the going would get tougher.

▼ **Magazine cover,** *Record Mirror*, **England, 23 December 1967.**

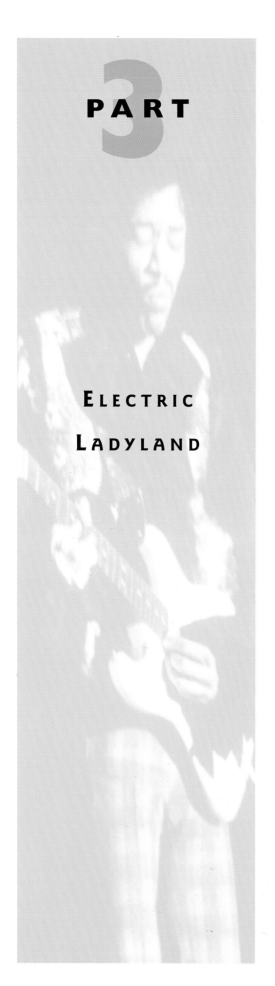

# PART 3

# ELECTRIC LADYLAND

Per Magnusson left his desk at the hotel Opalen and went to investigate a complaint about the noise from one of the rooms. Letting himself into Mitch Mitchell's room, Magnusson found chairs overturned, the curtain torn, the window smashed and blood everywhere – the only thing left unscathed was the telephone. And lying on the bed was a dishevelled-looking Jimi Hendrix with Mitch trying to calm him down. 'These crazy pop stars!' thought Magnusson. He had seen enough – this was a matter for the police.

The Experience had flown into Sweden at the beginning of January 1968 for a short four-date tour. Having checked into the hotel, Jimi and Mitch decided to sample the local nightlife and had had a few drinks. Returning in the early hours, Jimi was a little drunk and the worse for wear. According to Noel, Jimi had been hanging out with a gay Swedish journalist, who had been getting on everyone's nerves. Later, Mitch heard Jimi causing a commotion in the landing. Trying to calm him down, Mitch took Jimi back into his room, but Jimi started to smash Mitch's room up.

▶ **Poster which came with the magazine *Go Girl* (England), January 1968.**

◄ **These shots were taken just moments before Jimi went onstage to perform in concert at Lorensberg Cirkus, Göteborg, Sweden.**
*4 January 1968*

▲ **Jimi can smile again after leaving the Municipal Court in Göteborg, Sweden.**
*16 January 1968*

▲ **LP, Polydor, England – re-release.**

▲ **CD, Reprise, USA, 1989 – re-release.**

Jimi was charged with criminal damage, and Chas Chandler smoothed things over with the hotel by paying for repairs. Mitch thought Jimi had lost his temper with someone wanting to hang out with him, when all Jimi wanted to do was go to sleep or be left alone. Normally, Jimi was a respectful and gentle person who drank only in moderation if at all; back in his days with The Tom Cats, he was known to be a teetotaller and a non-smoker – when the rest of the band disappeared during breaks for a quick drink and cigarette, Jimi would stay behind and practice. Not being used to alcohol, after several drinks Jimi's temper could get the better of him. It was ironic that Jimi's consumption of illegal drugs such as cannabis and LSD seldom (if at all) affected him for the worse, whereas alcohol could knock him straight off his feet.

Once they settled their differences with the Swedish authorities and completed their remaining European concert dates, the Experience again returned to the States on 30 January 1968. Sales of the band's first two albums had been encouraging in America, and would be boosted by what would be the Experience's first US headline tour. Besides, in the States they could make better money than in Europe, which definitely appealed to Michael Jeffery.

Experience gigs and equipment problems almost always seemed to go hand in hand, and this tour wasn't an exception. Jimi was now using Fender amplification, and he struggled in vain to get his sound from the amps – they weren't loud enough, nor did they offer enough distortion. At the beginning of the second show in Anaheim on 9 February, an amp fused and Jimi couldn't hide his frustration, missing out words from songs and leaving the stage early. Backstage, Noel again berated Jimi for his lack of professionalism.

The band obtained Sunn amps, but the company was unable to comprehend Jimi's amplification requirements. Their engineers disapproved of Jimi playing with everything on 'ten', so they redesigned their amps so that when Jimi put the volume control on 'ten' he was only getting what would normally be a 'six'- or 'seven'-volume level. 'Where's the distortion? Where's the sustain?' Jimi must have wondered. He wasn't fooled by this, and returned to the Marshall equipment – although it wasn't totally reliable, at least he could get closer to the sounds he wanted.

The road eventually led back to Seattle, just as it had done when Jimi was playing with the Isley Brothers. Jimi hadn't seen his father nor the rest of his family for nearly seven years, and had kept in touch only sporadically by letter or telephone. Jimi was now a famous rock star, but there had been big changes in Al's life as well – he had remarried, and now had a step-daughter. 'I'm afraid to go home,' Jimi said. 'My father is a very strict man. He would immediately take a hold of me, tear my current clothes off my body and cut my hair quite thoroughly.' Jimi needn't have worried – Al didn't pull out a pair of scissors at the airport, but instead introduced Jimi to Ayako, his second wife, and Janie, Jimi's new stepsister. Mitch recalled that Jimi had been apprehensive about the reunion, but Al 'was obviously delighted to see his

► Jimi and Lulu photographed together for an article in *Disc and Music Echo* (England), 17 February 1968, celebrating their respective awards in the polls. Jimi was voted 'Top musician of the world'.

◄ Attractive poster which came with the Reprise, USA release of the *Smash Hits* LP in 1969.

▲ *Beat Instrumental* (England), April 1968.

and [...] doin[...] to th[...]

T[...] New[...] 1968[...] and [...] band[...] the s[...]

'[...] from[...] rem[...] beau[...] Mar[...] mus[...] no a[...] and [...] reco[...]

T[...] in N[...] mad[...] Ted[...] brea[...] Jimi[...] – sp[...] in si[...] the s[...] for t[...] new[...] *Hits*[...]

a damn what we were [...]g their eyes and listening [...] – they wanted action! [...]d themselves in Newark, [...] Luther King, on 4 April [...]d the city was stunned [...]e running high, and the [...]

MM EXCLUSIVE—HENDRIX IN NEW YORK

# The Black Elvis
## BY FRANK SIMPSON

▲ *Melody Maker* (England), 16 March 1968.

**THE IN SOUND**

Presented by the United States Army
For Broadcast Week of February 5, 1968

**FIVE MINUTE PROGRAMS**

SIDE ONE
MICROGROOVE          33-1/3 RPM

Band 1 - "WE CAN FLY"
            The Cowsills
        2 - "TALES OF BRAVE NEW ULYSSES"
            The Cream
        3 - "I'M IN LOVE"
            Wilson Pickett

**Host: HARRY HARRISON**

This record is the Property of the Government of the United States and must be used as Public Service Material only

USA-IS 81A

**I** Rare US Army LP from 1968. It contains a short radio interview with Noel Redding (with Jimi giggling in the background) plus the studio version of 'Foxy Lady'.

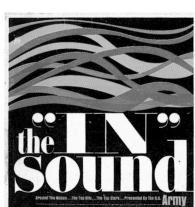

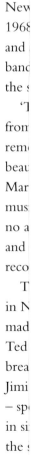

207    JIMI HENDRIX

The Experience weren't able to devote themselves to creating in the studio as they might have liked since they had to fly to Italy for a short tour at the end of May, followed by two dates in Zürich, Switzerland. The band then flew to England for an appearance on Dusty Springfield's TV show 'It Must Be Dusty!'. Their only other UK performance that year was headlining the Woburn Music Festival in July, followed by a date at the Sgt. Pepper's club in Majorca, Spain. The Experience stayed some extra days in Spain, enjoying a well-earned but brief holiday. Taking a rare break from music, Jimi went swimming in Bermuda shorts and flippers and also went go-kart racing.

### A BIT OF CLASSICAL BLUES

Although the break helped to refresh the Experience, Jimi had grown tired of playing in a three-piece band, and was keen to bring in additional musicians to augment the band's sound. However, this didn't go down well with Noel Redding. Mitch enjoyed working with other musicians, but even he saw that jamming in the studio surrounded by the sundry groupies and hangers-on that Jimi brought along was not a particularly effective way to work. And as for Chas.... He grew so frustrated by Jimi's desire to record songs over and over in pursuit of that elusive perfect take that he eventually walked out, leaving Jimi to produce most of the album with engineer Eddie Kramer's help.

More diverse than the Experience's first two albums, *Electric Ladyland* was an ambitious collection of songs that encompassed many different moods and musical styles, but still hung together as a cohesive whole. Originally packaged as a double LP set, *Electric Ladyland* was also considerably longer than the Experience's first two albums, with a playing time of over seventy minutes. *Electric Ladyland* began with 'a ninety-second sound painting of the heavens,' similar in style and execution to 'EXP' from *Axis: Bold As Love*, but displaying greater finesse and sophistication. The almost-title track of 'Have You Ever Been (To Electric Ladyland)?' saw Jimi returning to the chord/melody style of playing he had featured on *Axis: Bold As Love*, but with an even greater sense of musical sophistication, something which can also be heard in the chord progression of 'Crosstown Traffic'.

The first real musical departure on *Electric Ladyland* came with 'Voodoo Chile'. Eschewing the three-piece Jimi Hendrix Experience format, Jimi drafted in Steve Winwood from Traffic on organ and bassist Jack Casady from Jefferson Airplane for this spontaneous slow blues. 'There were no chord sheets. He just started playing. It was a one-take job, with him singing and playing at the same time,' said Winwood. The applause heard on the track was added later via an overdub, appropriately reflecting the live feel of the track.

◄▲ Poster and program magazine for the 'Pop-Monsterkonzert' in Zürich, 1968. Mini-riots broke out on the second day after the concert, due to excessive force used by the Swiss police.

◄ The day the stars came out – from left to right: Eric Burdon (Animals), Stu Leathwood (Koobas), Keith Ellis (Koobas), Roy Wood (Move), Jimi Hendrix, Noel Redding, Carl Wayne (Move), John Mayall, Steve Winwood (Traffic), Trevor Burton (Move), Roy Morris (Koobas).

*Zürich, Switzerland, 31 May 1968*

Always with an ear for new sounds, in 'House Burning Down', Jimi used studio effects to make his guitar sound as if it were on fire, and in '1983... (A Merman I Should Turn To Be)' he used feedback from his headphones to imitate the sound of seagulls. As Eddie Kramer commented, 'He had a fantastic mind for colour and space and timing – his timing was immaculate.' '1983' was one of Jimi's most ambitious compositions, blending backwards guitar parts, his sound painting technique and a pseudo-classical structure. 'I like to break away and do a bit of classical blues,' explained Jimi. 'I want to get into what you'd call "pieces" behind each other to make movements.'

The penultimate track on *Electric Ladyland* was Jimi's masterful reading of Dylan's 'All Along The Watchtower'. Dylan was so impressed by Jimi's interpretation that 'ever since he died I've been doing it the same way.' 'Voodoo Child (slight return)' closed the album, making reference to the earlier 'Voodoo Chile' and adding to the album's overall feel of unity. 'Somebody was filming us as we started doing that,' explained Jimi. 'It was like, OK, boys, look like you're recording. It was in the studio and they were recording it... so it was one-two-three and then we went into "Voodoo Child".'

The album title *Electric Ladyland* partly referred to groupies whom Jimi had a great deal of respect for. 'Some groupies know more about music than the guys.... Some people call them groupies, but I prefer the term "Electric Ladies".' Unfortunately, Track Records didn't grasp the reverence in this concept, and covered the double-album sleeve with a photo of twenty-one nude models. And it was not a very flattering photo, either – one of the models commented that 'It makes us look like a load of old prostitutes.' Much to Jimi's frustration, the UK release on 25 October 1968 of what is widely regarded as his finest recorded work met with almost as much controversy over the cover as discussion of the music. Thankfully, in America, Reprise Records used a record sleeve which was more in line with Jimi's wishes.

Although Jimi complained about the record's production, he pronounced, 'I'm happy with the content of the record.' And so were the critics. In his review entitled 'The Hendrix religion' for *The Observer*, Tony Palmer said, 'Track Records have a major triumph on their hands not only commercially, but, more importantly, artistically, for each record is, in its different way, a pop work of genius.' Sure enough, *Electric Ladyland* reached number five in the UK charts, and in the States the Experience were rewarded for their almost non-stop touring with their first number-one album in the charts.

## (THEM) CHANGES

Jimi's greatest artistic achievement didn't come without a price, though. Now that Jimi had taken on the role of producer in the studio, Chas had felt there was no point in staying, and some time later Michael Jeffery bought him out. Although Jimi and Chas had clashed in the studio when recording *Electric Ladyland*, as a former gigging and recording musician Chas was still closer to Jimi's music than Michael.

However, even though Michael excelled in tricky negotiations, he couldn't free Jimi from his PPX contract with Ed Chalpin. Jimi dismissed the

◀ **Rare colour photograph of Jimi playing a black Gibson Les Paul.**
*Hallenstadion, Zürich, Switzerland, 31 May 1968*

1 Single, Track, England, 1969.

2 Sheet music, England, 1969.

3 Single, Polydor, Germany, 1969.

4 Single, Polydor, Japan, 1969.

Curtis Knight records on which he played as 'crap'; he was disappointed that his old friend Curtis Knight had let him down, and annoyed that Ed Chalpin had broken his word not to release his jams with Knight. Jimi's popularity meant that Chalpin was on to a winner, and Warner Bros. (who owned Reprise Records) were scared to challenge the fairness of Jimi's PPX contract in court in case a lengthy legal dispute would prevent Warners from releasing Jimi Hendrix material when he was hot property. A deal was worked out whereby Chalpin would be given Jimi's fourth album, plus a 2 per cent royalty on the Jimi Hendrix Experience's first three albums. Chalpin was still free to release Jimi's jams with Curtis Knight, and was free to sue Track and Polydor in Britain – he could hardly have wished for a better outcome.

As *Electric Ladyland* was being released, the Experience found themselves back on the road in America and returned to San Francisco in October to play three nights at Winterland, performing two shows a night. The audience in San Francisco was known to be particularly open-minded, and they wouldn't pester Jimi by yelling out 'Wild Thing' between every song nor demand to see Jimi smash his guitar.

For the first night, bassist Jack Casady joined the Experience onstage – Casady had played on 'Voodoo Chile' on *Electric Ladyland*. On the second night, flutist Virgil Gonzales pla⎯ ⎯n 'Are You Experienced?' in the first set and organist Herb ⎯ ⎯ich joined the band for several songs in the second set. Jimi al⎯ ⎯ changed the way he approached songs, using them as a springboard for longer, looser improvisations, as can be heard on the posthumous release *Live At Winter*⎯ ⎯ (1987), compiled from these six Winterland shows.

No matter how hectic and complicated his life might be offstage, Jimi could always take refuge in the blues – so for the third song in the first set of the first night at Winterland, Jimi led the Experience into his blues 'Red House.' 'Most people believe that to be a good blues musician one has to suffer. I don't believe this. When I hear certain notes I feel real happy.' Jimi's original 'Red House' from *Are You Experienced?* clocked in at a modest three minutes and forty seconds, whereas 'Red House' from the first night at Winterland reached a staggering fourteen minutes, as can be heard on *Variations On A Theme: Red House* (1989). Playing one of their slowest and longest versions of 'Red House', Jimi led Noel and Mitch through a variety of musical moods and colours, showing an astounding control of dynamics ranging from a raucous, double-time gallop goaded on by his screaming guitar to the most gentle and sensitive of slow, laid-back blues.

Elsewhere, audiences were not so broad-minded. As Jimi said, 'What can you do on a tour? People scream for the oldies but goodies. So you have to play the oldies but goo⎯⎯⎯ your show instead of some of the things you want to get into. Plus we don⎯⎯⎯e – we never practise! We've practised about three times since we've been together.' Some of the 'oldies', like 'Hey Joe', had become a chore to play, but audiences expected to hear them, so the Experience arrived at a compromise by playing different arrangements.

▲ **Cutting from magazine *Top Pops* (England), late 1968.**

▲ **Double LP, Polydor, Germany, 1987.**

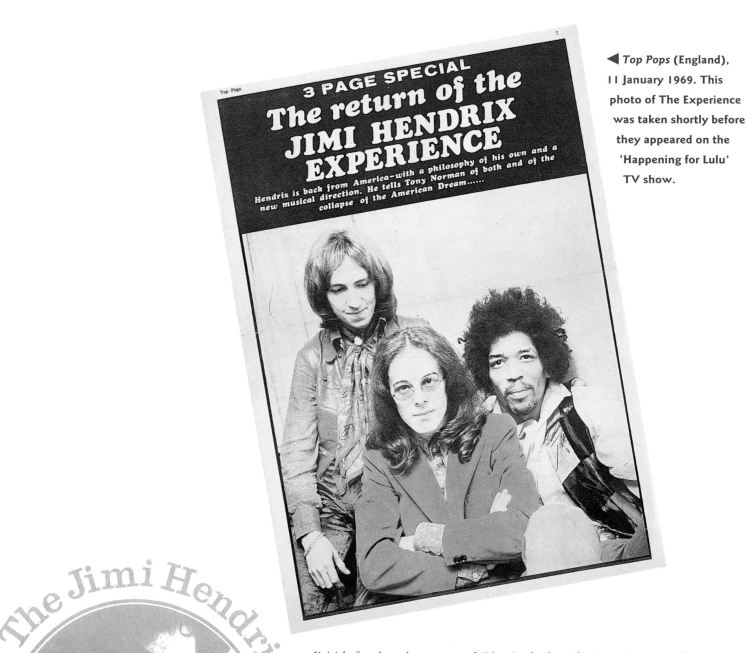

Top Pops

**3 PAGE SPECIAL**

# The return of the JIMI HENDRIX EXPERIENCE

Hendrix is back from America—with a philosophy of his own and a new musical direction. He tells Tony Norman of both and of the collapse of the American Dream......

◀ *Top Pops* (England), 11 January 1969. This photo of The Experience was taken shortly before they appeared on the 'Happening for Lulu' TV show.

British fans heard a revamped 'Hey Joe' when the Experience made an appearance on Lulu's UK TV show 'Happening For Lulu' on 4 January 1969. Introducing the Experience, Lulu gamely took a stray burst of feedback from Jimi's guitar in her stride. Jimi led the band into 'Hey Joe', attacking the vibrato arm with his customary vigour but leaving his guitar out of tune. As he sang the first verse, Jimi hit a glorious bum note, but coolly retuned his bottom string and smiled over to Mitch. Unexpectedly, Jimi brought the song to a premature halt, then stepped up to the mic.

'We'd like to stop playing this rubbish and dedicate a song to the Cream,' Jimi announced, then took the band into Cream's 'Sunshine Of Your Love', totally unplanned. Broadcast as live TV, the producer was making threatening gestures to the band from behind the camera – the show was ending, but not in the way it was supposed to! Taunting the producer even further, Jimi announced to the viewers, 'We're being put off the air!', barely able to contain his obvious glee. 'We didn't know anything about it!' admitted Mitch. 'But it didn't surprise us – that's the kind of wicked humour that he had.'

## ON THE ROAD

The day before 'Happening For Lulu', Jimi and Kathy Etchingham had moved into a flat at 23 Brook Street in London – next door to the classical composer Handel's previous residence at number 25. Jimi and Kathy had barely settled in when Jimi had to leave because the Experience were on the road again in Europe. Chas came to see the band in Göteborg, and Jimi asked him to come back and manage the band – but Chas refused. The Experience moved on to Germany, where Jimi met an ice skating teacher called Monika Dannemann. She had seen the Experience concert in Düsseldorf on 12 January with her younger brother, Klaus-Peter. After the concert, Monika and Klaus-Peter were invited to join the Experience in a club, but Monika declined the invitation since she was simply not interested in meeting 'famous people', and was also wary of Jimi's 'wild man' media image. But one of Monika's friends persuaded her to bring her camera the next morning to the hotel where the Experience were staying to take some photos, and Monika finally met Jimi. Expecting a fast-living, arrogant rock star, Monika was surprised by the person she met – 'I realised he was a very gentle, kind person, very considerate' – and they spent some time together chatting and getting to know each other.

'Within two hours he had managed to turn my life upside down, and it would never be the same again.' Although they had only just met, Monika said that Jimi felt they had known each other for a long time and were

▲ Collection of bootleg CDs, all containing material from the six Experience shows at Winterland in San Francisco during October 1968.

destined to be together. That evening whilst driving to Köln to meet Jimi backstage at the Sporthalle, Monika realized she had fallen in love with Jimi.

Michael Jeffery had pushed up the Experience's concert fees to the point where practically the only places that could afford to book them were large stadiums in America. However, the Experience were booked to play two shows in London's Royal Albert Hall, a very prestigious venue, in February 1969. Not in the mood to play, Jimi almost had to be pushed on stage for their first concert on the 18th of February, and he consequently gave a very restrained performance.

**▲ Rheinhalle, Düsseldorf, Germany.**
*12 January 1969, 2nd show*

'Yeah, we'll be, uh, just jamming, you know...' said Jimi at the beginning of the second concert on 24 February. The Experience stretched out 'Stone Free' to well over ten minutes, Jimi drawing on a seemingly endless stream of musical ideas in his guitar solo, this track being later released on *The Jimi Hendrix Concerts* (1989), although in a slightly incomplete form. Jimi played the blues 'Red House' on a Gibson SG Custom rather than a Fender Stratocaster, getting a 'tougher' tone than usual and playing some particularly jazz-influenced chords, as can be heard on *Variations On A Theme: Red House* (1989). Later in the set, the band were joined onstage by Chris Wood on flute for a lengthy jam on a new song still in development called 'Room Full Of Mirrors'. The Experience normally played for fifty-five minutes, but the jamming in this concert made it almost one and a half hours long.

On 13 March Jimi flew to New York City, leaving behind Kathy Etchingham in the rented Brook Street residence they had briefly shared. She followed him to New York afterwards, but according to roadie Eric Barrett, 'Jimi doesn't want anything to do with her. He left her in England, she followed him over on her own money.' Jimi helped her to find a room when she arrived in New York, but as far as he was concerned, their relationship had ended.

After a much-needed break, the Experience were back on the road in the States, and on 3 May they flew into Toronto airport for the evening's show at the Maple Leaf Gardens. Officer Marvin Wilson asked to see Jimi's flight bag at customs. Wilson looked into the bag and brought out a metal tube stained with a dark resin and three small packets of a white powder.

Hash stains and heroin – Jimi couldn't believe it! Everyone knew it was far too risky to carry drugs through customs, and the Experience had been specifically warned that there might be trouble at Toronto airport. Besides, Jimi didn't even take heroin – Kathy Etchingham said that Jimi had experimented with heroin, but it had made him sick so he didn't try it again. Jimi was charged and released on bail pending a trial by jury. Despite everything that had happened earlier that day, the Experience still turned in a good performance at the concert that evening.

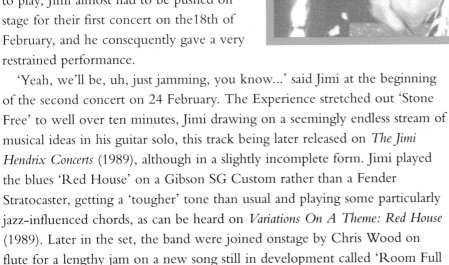

**◄ Jimi with his black Fender Stratocaster (aka 'Black Beauty').**
*Konserthuset, Copenhagen, Denmark, 10 January 1969*

▲ **Afternoon rehearsals at the Royal Albert Hall, London, 24 February 1969.**

1 'Souvenir Brochure', sold during the two Royal Albert Hall concerts in London on 18 and 24 February 1969.

2 Bootleg LP containing material from the Royal Albert Hall performances.

3 Another bootleg from Japan – a different title, but containing the same songs from the Royal Albert Hall performances.

The impending trial cast a long, dark shadow over Jimi's summer, but the Experience were still able to rise to the occasion and turn in some good shows. Back in Seattle on 23 May 1969 for a show at the Coliseum, the reviewer from the *Seattle Times* made an acute observation about Jimi's apparent 'oneness' with his guitar: 'Hendrix's guitar seemed to be an extension of his body; the peculiar positions from which he sometimes played seemed a result of emotion – as if just to hold the guitar normally could not express his erupting feelings. The impression was that if Hendrix were to have put down his guitar, the music would have to come from his body – that the instrument was entirely superfluous.'

As the summer progressed, the Experience played at the Mile End Stadium in Denver on 29 June 1969, the headline act of the three-day festival. Unfortunately, this festival erupted into violence; fights broke out between the police and the gatecrashers, with the police making excessive use of tear gas. But Jimi was having a beautiful time as he'd dropped some good acid before he went onstage.

Towards the end of the show, Jimi stepped up to the microphone, and suddenly announced: 'Yeah, this is the last time we're playing....'

▼ **Taken during a concert at the Maple Leaf Gardens, Toronto, Ontario, Canada.**
*3 May 1969*

◄ **Cutting from** *Melody Maker* **(England),**
*5 July 1969*

HENDRIX AND REDDING, parting company

# Hendrix split: Redding goes, group grows

**PLANS** by Jimi Hendrix to enlarge his Experience have led to British bass guitarist Noel Redding quitting the group.

Noel decided to end his association with Hendrix, begun in September 1967, last weekend. The crux of the split, it appears, is that he was not consulted by Jimi over his plans to expand the group from a trio into a "creative commune" which would include writers as well as more musicians.

Chas Chandler, ex-manager and record producer of the Experience, said at presstime that Noel was expected to return to London from the States at the end of this week to discuss his future.

Said Chandler: "Obviously it is too early to make any statement until we have had a chance to sit down and work things out, but there are a lot of exciting possibilities for Noel."

When he was last in London, Noel said he expected to stay with the Experience until Septem-

## MITCH MITCHELL'S PLANS UNKNOWN

ber, at least.

It is not yet known whether drummer Mitch Mitchell will remain with Hendrix or also return to Britain.

Noel Redding's own group, Fat Mattress, have been set for the 9th National Jazz And Blues Festival — renamed the London Jazz Blues And Pop Festival — at West Drayton, Middlesex, on Saturday, August 9 (see Page 2).

Hendrix is currently reported to be grossing over 100,000 dollars a night on his appearances in the States.

The Hendrix Experience last played in Britain in February when they gave a sell-out concert at the Royal Albert Hall.

MITCHELL: may return

◄ **Whenever Jimi was in London, he would hang out at the Speakeasy club and participate in jam sessions. Here Jimi is pictured during a jam with a band called The Gods.**
*Mid-March 1969*

# GYPSY SUN
# AND RAINBOWS

"WE DECIDED TO CHANGE A LITTLE THING AROUND AND
CALL IT 'GYPSY SUN AND RAINBOWS'.
FOR SHORT, IT'S NOTHING BUT A BAND OF GYPSIES."

*JIMI HENDRIX*

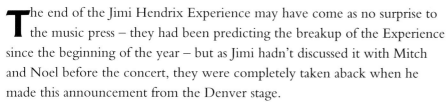

▲ **Three completely different items, but all bearing the same title – the book** *Electric Church: A Visual Experience* **(top/left), sold at Hendrix concerts in America during Spring 1969; LP (top/right) by the Buddy Miles Express released by Mercury, USA, 1968 (for which Jimi produced four songs); and finally, a bootleg LP with a live Jimi Hendrix Experience show from Copenhagen, Denmark, 10 January 1969. (By coincidence, one presumes, the manufacturer of this bootleg is now a born-again Christian.)**

◄ **Action shot from Lorensberg Cirkus, Göteborg, Sweden.**
*8 January 1969*

T he end of the Jimi Hendrix Experience may have come as no surprise to the music press – they had been predicting the breakup of the Experience since the beginning of the year – but as Jimi hadn't discussed it with Mitch and Noel before the concert, they were completely taken aback when he made this announcement from the Denver stage.

'I can't play guitar any more the way, eh, I want to. You know, I get very frustrated sometimes on stage, when we play. I think it's because it's only three pieces, you know. I like to work with other things too, and I'm sure they would too, you know. But that doesn't necessarily mean we have to break the group up, you know.' Jimi had been nursing plans to assemble a larger and more flexible group of musicians, which he occasionally referred to as 'Electric Church'. Jimi wanted to be freed from the constraints imposed by a three-piece line-up so that he could experiment with different musical ideas and different musicians.

To this end, Jimi retreated to a country mansion near the village of Shokan, near Woodstock, New York, and began contacting musicians to come and join him. His superstar status meant there would be no shortage of musicians wanting to play with him, but Jimi had grown wary of people's motives now that he was a rich and famous rock star. So, Jimi looked to his past and asked his old friend Billy Cox to come join him and play bass.

▲ **The perfect Benson & Hedges advertisement! — Jimi recording at the Hit Factory, New York.**

*Late August, 1969*

Musically, Cox was a solid and dependable player but, just as important, Jimi had known Cox since his army days, and their warm friendship gave Jimi a sense of continuity in his ever-changing and hectic life. Although Jimi was meeting new people all the time, at the end of the day he had few close friends on whom he could rely.

A more surprising choice was bringing in Larry Lee to play guitar in the band. Another face from Jimi's past, Larry had befriended and helped Jimi when he was a struggling, penniless musician in Nashville. Just back from Vietnam, Larry was unemployed and was putting his life back together when Jimi and Billy called him on the phone and asked if he wanted to join them. Larry needed little persuasion, but confessed to being a little apprehensive – as a competent but unspectacular guitarist, playing alongside Jimi Hendrix was hardly the best way to make the transition back to 'normality' after serving his time in Vietnam!

Jimi wanted to break away from the relentless pounding of the power-trio format of the Experience, so he brought not one but two percussionists – Jerry Velez and Juma Sultan. After some uncertainty about who would play the drums, eventually Mitch Mitchell joined the rehearsals at Shokan and the band started practising for their eagerly anticipated Woodstock festival debut, which was scheduled for Sunday 17 August 1969 – the last day of the festival.

'Three days of Peace and Music' proclaimed the posters for the Woodstock Music And Art Fair. Instead, according to Mitch, it was three days of 'mud, no food, no toilets and exhaustion.' Nevertheless, Woodstock was arguably the major counterculture 'happening' of the sixties, crystallizing the sixties' dream that people could co-exist peacefully together, albeit for only three days.

Michael Jeffery had insisted that Jimi was to headline the festival by going on last. Unfortunately, the circular stage had broken down, and band changeovers were taking so long that the program was running way behind schedule. Jimi didn't start his set until around eight o' clock on Monday

morning. By this time, many of the audience had left, and as Jimi took the stage he could see tiny figures in the distance making their weary way home – hardly the best of welcomings.

Introduced as 'the Jimi Hendrix Experience', Jimi was keen to set the record straight. 'We decided to change a little thing around and call it "Gypsy Sun And Rainbows". For short, it's nothing but a band of gypsies,' said Jimi before introducing the individual members of the band in a true democratic fashion. 'We only had about two rehearsals, so....' Gypsy Sun And Rainbows played a loose set, with Billy and Mitch providing a solid bottom for a strong performance from Jimi, but the full potential of the line-up remained untapped due to the lack of rehearsals.

A few days before Woodstock, Jimi complemented his onstage set-up with a Uni-Vibe unit. This effect added a rich, 'warbling' sound to Jimi's guitar, as can be heard in his rendition of 'The Star Spangled Banner' on the *Woodstock* LP. If any one song could be said to have captured the spirit of Woodstock, it was 'The Star Spangled Banner'. Although this was by no means Jimi's first performance of America's national anthem, it was one of his strongest, with his notoriously unpredictable sound coming together perfectly to make a memorable musical and political statement. Jimi used amplifier feedback, his effects and the vibrato arm on his guitar to conjure up the sounds of warfare, which he then incorporated into the melody of 'The Star Spangled Banner'.

Jimi's use of programmatic music in which sounds are used to illustrate non-musical ideas is virtually unparalleled by any other rock musician, and his treatment of 'The Star Spangled Banner' was widely interpreted as an anti-Vietnam statement. Jimi was more diplomatic about his motives when interviewed on Dick Cavett's US TV program on 9 September: 'I thought it was beautiful, but there you go,' said Jimi before flashing a peace sign at the camera, leaving the viewers free to make their own interpretations.

Although Jimi's Woodstock performance is best remembered for 'The Star Spangled Banner', it wasn't the only high point of the Gypsy Sun And Rainbows set, as he also played a particularly powerful version of 'Voodoo Child (slight return)'. Jimi also did a largely unaccompanied piece known as 'Instrumental Solo', in which he improvised a constant stream of musical ideas for nearly five minutes, including ferocious blues licks, flamenco-influenced passages and sophisticated rhythm guitar patterns. 'Instrumental Solo' segued into the premiere of a beautifully laid-back instrumental called 'Villanova Junction Blues'.

Michael Jeffery could see that Jimi didn't need two percussionists and a rhythm guitarist to turn in a good show. If anything, they succeeded in diverting attention from the star of the performance, and Jerry, Juma and

▲ Bootleg LP picture disc from 1993. Despite the concert photo taken at Woodstock, it contained only studio outtakes.

▲ Parts of Jimi's concert at Woodstock were released on the above LP sets (Cotillion, USA, 1970 and 1971 respectively).

◀ **'Woodstock Music
And Art Fair', Bethel,
New York.**
*18 August 1969*

Larry began to get the distinct impression that they weren't wanted – Juma claimed his congas were thrown around by roadies, and Larry was not allowed to play on the 'Dick Cavett Show' because 'they wanted to keep the image steady.'

## CROSSTOWN TRAFFIC

However, Gypsy Sun And Rainbows' fragile line-up wasn't Jimi's only worry – he was keen to break his ties with the money-grabbing Michael Jeffery, but couldn't see an easy way out. Jimi knew that he had earned a vast sum of money over the past three years, but he suspected that his financial affairs were in a mess, and was even worried that he might be liable for a huge tax bill. An additional expense which would drain Jimi's finances was the building of a recording studio, Electric Lady, which Michael and Jimi had commissioned. Intended primarily for Jimi's own use, the studio would eliminate Jimi's ever-growing studio bills caused by block-booking sessions in expensive studios.

Meanwhile, Jimi was being hassled by the Black Panthers, a militant black activists' group who wanted Jimi to help with their cause. Jimi had been a victim of prejudice against blacks such as New York cab drivers refusing to have him in their cabs simply because of the colour of his skin. 'Dat piece of black shit in the girlies' hat – get out of my cab!' was the welcome Jimi received from one cab driver. Mitch Mitchell recalled that when the Experience were in the Deep South on tour with the Monkees back in '67, Jimi would refuse to go into certain shops and restaurants with Mitch and Noel because of the racial tension. However, Mitchell also recalled one occasion in which the Experience were being chauffeured by a member of the Ku Klux Klan. Did Jimi cower in the backseat? Certainly not – Jimi made a point out of sitting in the front of the limo, just to show the driver who the boss was!

Jimi had little time for militancy on either side of the racial divide. He was fond of saying 'I'm not from this planet', and saw himself as a citizen of the world – or the universe! – rather than a black man in a white man's world. But Jimi never disowned his black roots, and he was hurt when he was called a 'white nigger' or a 'coconut' (black outside, white inside) by some activists. Yet despite this pressure, Jimi still didn't feel it was appropriate for him to act as a spokesman for black America, nor did he feel it was necessary to surround himself with black musicians. Five of the six people in Gypsy Sun And Rainbows may have been black, but Jimi never intended this to be a racial statement.

The second Gypsy Sun And Rainbows gig was played in an altogether less peaceful and loving atmosphere than Woodstock. The Salvation in New York was only a small club venue, but Michael Jeffery wanted Jimi to play there as a gesture of goodwill to the Mafia who ran the club. The Mafia were concerned about the location of Electric Lady Studios in an area they 'controlled' and the possible increase of police interest in the area that might follow when the studio opened.

Reluctantly, Jimi agreed to play. However, the audience were expecting to see the 'wild man of rock' act with the flashy guitar tricks and the smashed

**THE STAR SPANGLED BANNER**
as performed at Woodstock
by Jimi Hendrix
plus
**WOODEN SHIPS** by Crosby, Stills, Nash & Young
(See CSN on tour this summer in support of their upcoming Atlantic LP!)
&
**FREEDOM** by Richie Havens

In celebration of Woodstock's 25th Anniversary, The Best Of Woodstock also features Hendrix's "Purple Haze" and legendary live performances by The Who, Jefferson Airplane, Santana, Joe Cocker, John Sebastian, Canned Heat, Country Joe McDonald, Joan Baez and Ten Years After.

PRCD 5712

▲ **Promo CD, Atlantic, USA, 1991.**

▲ **Afros in motion – Benefit concert for the United Block Association.**
*Harlem, New York, 5 September 1969*

equipment. They were disappointed – Jimi had long since tired of this act and was determined to concentrate on the music, leading the band through a series of songs left open for extended improvising and sharing the guitar soloing duties with Larry Lee. The reviewer from *Rock* magazine commented, 'It was sad to see Hendrix, creating a series of superb informal compositions, being condemned by a horde of ten-dollar-paying customers who finally chose to walk out.'

Things were little better for Gypsy Sun And Rainbows in the studio, as jazz producer Alan Douglas observed when Jimi invited him to the studio. Alan got a shock when he arrived: 'It was close to midnight when we left for the Record Plant. Everyone else turned up about two hours later. I never saw such disorganization in all of my life. No one in either the control room or the studio was taking care of business for him.' Alan could clearly see that Jimi needed guidance in the studio, but he also saw that Jimi was being frustrated in his musical goals by the musicians he was working with – something that Michael Jeffery, as a non-musician, failed to grasp.

Alan suggested Jimi ought to broaden his horizons and play with jazz musicians, and even tried to organize a session with Miles Davis – unfortunately, Miles wouldn't play with Jimi in the studio for less than $50,000. However, Miles claimed that Jimi went round to his house and the two of them jammed together in private. Although Alan Douglas only worked with Jimi in the studio for around two months, in the years after Jimi's death, Douglas exerted a huge influence over his legacy.

Despite Jimi's desire to play in a more relaxed musical setting after the break-up of the Experience, it was clear that the Gypsy Sun And Rainbows line-up was not going to gel as a musical unit, so Jimi effectively disbanded the group after only two gigs.

# BAND OF GYPSYS

"The music I might hear I can't get on the guitar...
I can't play my guitar that well to get all this music together!"

*Jimi Hendrix*

▶ **Band of Gypsys concert at the Fillmore East in New York City.**

*31 December 1969*

E d Chalpin was nothing if not persistent, and he began to press Jimi for a new album – the fourth Jimi Hendrix Experience album that Warner Bros. had decided he was entitled to under the PPX contract. Michael Jeffery wanted to get Chalpin off their backs, and with his keen sense of business acumen, it didn't take long for Jeffery to realize that a live recording would be a convenient way to fulfil the obligation – a live record would have low production costs, and it would be much quicker to record than a studio album. And as for Jimi's musical integrity, well.... Jeffery was frequently more concerned with money than music. There was one problem though – Jimi didn't have a band to play with!

Mitch Mitchell was asked to join Jimi for the recordings, but as he didn't want to leave his new house in England, Buddy Miles from Michael Bloomfield's Electric Flag took the drum stool. Billy Cox had played with Jimi at Woodstock and in recent studio sessions, so he was the natural choice as bassist. Jimi had been under pressure from various sources to play with black musicians and to take more of a political stand on black issues, and the formation of the Band of Gypsys with three black musicians was seen by some as a sign of bowing to this pressure. However, since Mitch Mitchell had been asked to join as a drummer before Buddy Miles, the all-black line-up was a coincidence rather than a premeditated political act on Jimi's part.

### MACHINE GUN

Jimi regarded the Band of Gypsys as only a temporary unit, and his confused musical direction was further confounded by problems in his personal life. At this stage in his career, Jimi was struggling to harness his many musical ideas and to find the right musicians to achieve his musical goals. On top of that, drugs such as cannabis and LSD had once been a mind-expanding and fun way to relax, but now Jimi had started using cocaine, which led to feelings of paranoia. He wasn't happy with the way his career was being managed, and his girlfriend at the time, Devon Wilson, was getting beyond the point of no return with her heroin addiction. And if this wasn't enough, there was another drug-related affair looming on the horizon.

Jimi had been busted for drug possession earlier in the year in Toronto under curious circumstances – the police seemed to be expecting to bust him, and Jimi had been warned beforehand to expect trouble. A set-up to get Jimi Hendrix, the famous black rock star known to use drugs, who had so far eluded the police? It's not improbable. Another possibility is that the drugs were planted by a spurned male groupie – Jimi was known to have an almost insatiable sexual appetite, but he didn't show any bisexual tendencies.

On 6 December, two days before the start of Jimi's trial, a young black man was killed by the Hell's Angels at the Altamont Pop festival as the Rolling Stones played 'Sympathy For The Devil'. The 60s' dream of peace, love and understanding was turning into a nightmare. Jimi was especially depressed to hear the news while he was worrying about his imminent trial, and couldn't help but see this tragic incident as a bad omen. If he were to be found guilty and given the maximum seven-year prison sentence.... Jimi Hendrix's musical career would probably be over by the time he was released.

▲ Announcement in magazine *RAT* (USA), 25 December 1969.

▼ Fascinating drawing inspired by Jimi's song 'Machine Gun' – magazine *Rock & Folk* (France), 1975.

Always a flamboyant dresser, Jimi had to buy sober clothes specially for the trial. In 'If Six Was Nine' from *Axis: Bold As Love*, Jimi had asserted his individuality with 'I'm gonna wave my freak flag high' – but there was no freak flag waving on this day! In court, Jimi told the jury that he regularly received gifts from fans – including drugs – and he often didn't have time to examine them closely. The prosecutor presented Jimi with the metal tube in which some of the drugs were found, and asked if Mr Hendrix would please describe what it was to the jury. Jimi's response was, 'Probably a pea shooter!'

The court erupted with laughter. Jimi's genuinely innocent reply couldn't help but endear him to the jury. Fortunately for Jimi, after an eight-hour recess he was found not guilty. 'It's the best Christmas present Canada has ever given me', said Jimi as he held his hand in a 'V' for victory salute at the press gathering after the verdict.

On New Year's Eve 1969/1970, the Band of Gypsys made their highly anticipated debut at the Fillmore East in New York, booked by Bill Graham to play two nights. Mike Jahn reviewed the first night for the *New York Times*: 'Jimi Hendrix, a New Year's Eve noisemaker if ever there was one, played to a capacity crowd Wednesday night at the Fillmore East. The guitarist and singer plays what has been called "space rock". His playing is loud, so fluid and so rife with electronic distortions that it resembles that of no other currently popular performer. Mr Hendrix is less a tune weaver than a soundsmith. His bank of six amplifiers is turned up full blast. He seems as if he were moulding a living sculpture of sound rather than fulfilling the normal role of the entertainer.... He seems to be more concerned with creating an environment of intense sound and personal fury than he is with performing a particular composition.'

The Band of Gypsys played two sets each night, and all four sets were recorded for possible inclusion on the *Band Of Gypsys* album. While not of the same standard as the first three Jimi Hendrix Experience albums, *Band Of Gypsys* does contain some stunning playing. On 'Machine Gun', the album's most spectacular track, Jimi uses his guitar to imitate the sound of machine gun fire in a powerful anti-war statement echoing his treatment of 'The Star Spangled Banner' from Woodstock.

Jimi introduced 'Machine Gun' by saying, 'We'd like to dedicate this one to all the soldiers that are fighting in Chicago and Milwaukee and New York... Oh yes, and all the soldiers fighting in Vietnam.'

Although Jimi was too early to have been sent to Vietnam, he had nonetheless played his part in the conflict – many soldiers found solace from the horrors of Vietnam in Jimi's music. 'Machine Gun' is a musical tour-de-force of pure Hendrix – no

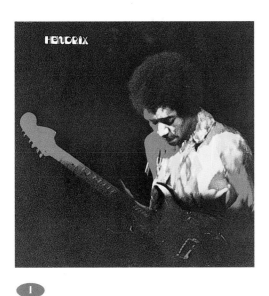

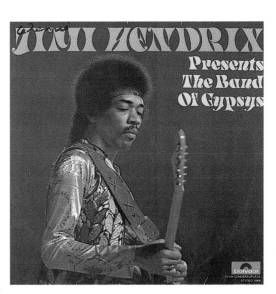

1. Live *Band Of Gypsys* LP, Capitol, USA, 1970.

2. Same LP, but now with the so-called 'puppet cover' –Track, England, 1970.

3. After the 'puppet cover' was withdrawn, Track replaced it with a photo of Jimi playing at the Isle of Wight festival on 30 August 1970.

4. Special edition – LP, Polydor, Germany, mid 70s.

5. More live material from the Band of Gypsys – LP, Capitol, USA, 1986.

▲ Advertisement from *The Village Voice*
(USA), 22 January 1970.

other guitarist could produce such a cohesive and yet fluid piece of music, ranging from savage and brutal to tender and full of sorrow. His control of the guitar sound and the 'warbling' sound of his Uni-Vibe effect, sustained for a full twelve minutes, perfectly complement the music and the sentiments of the lyrics.

There are other flashes of Jimi's guitar genius on *Band Of Gypsys*, such as his use of the Octavia pedal in 'Who Knows?', incorporating the strange, throaty, 'honking' sounds into his endlessly inventive solo. A perfunctory run through Buddy's uninspiring 'We Gotta Live Together' is rescued by Jimi's guitar playing, although Billy and Buddy fail to move up a gear with Jimi, who leaves them both plodding away in the background. Although the Band of Gypsys had rehearsed before the shows, Jimi admitted, 'We used to go and jam actually. We'd say "rehearsing" just to make it sound official.' Billy and Buddy provided a solid R&B-based rhythm section for Jimi to play over, but they lacked the flexibility and imagination to follow Jimi into new musical territories.

The original *Band Of Gypsys* release contained six songs, four written by Jimi and two by Buddy Miles. It could have easily been an all-Hendrix album, but it seems that either the perfectionist in Jimi preferred to record definitive versions of his new material in the studio before releasing them, or he wanted to be more democratic in the choice of songs. Whatever his reasoning behind the choice of songs, Jimi himself wasn't happy with the project: 'If it had been up to me, I would never have put it out. Not enough preparation went into it, and it came out a bit grizzly. The thing is, we owed the record company an album, and they were pushing us, so here it is.' Ed Chalpin eagerly accepted the album, but still complained that it wasn't as good as the Experience's first three albums. Nevertheless, the album was a commercial success, and went to the top five in the UK and the USA.

### EARTH BLUES

The Band of Gypsys' next performance was during a Madison Square Garden benefit concert at the end of January. It was terrible – one of Jimi's worst-ever concerts. One theory about Jimi's poor and distracted performance is that he was given some bad LSD before he played, perhaps by accident or perhaps intentionally. Michael Jeffery didn't like the Band of Gypsys line-up, but as he had hired a crew to film the gig, he is unlikely to have spiked Jimi; after the gig, Jimi said that Devon Wilson had spiked his drink to exercise control over him. Johnny Winter saw Jimi backstage before he played, and was shocked by what he saw: 'It was like he was already dead.'

Carlos Santana had made a similar observation about Jimi in the previous November, blaming it on the unhealthy lifestyle shared by many rock musicians of the time – over-indulgence in 'sex and drugs and rock 'n' roll'. Unlike many of the health-conscious and career-oriented rock musicians of the nineties, hedonistic lifestyles were the norm for many sixties rock stars. The guiding principal seemed to be 'have a good time, all the time', as later immortalized in the spoof 'rockumentary', 'This Is Spinal Tap'. Amusing in this context, it was certainly no joke to those who fell victim to this lifestyle.

As Santana himself commented, 'In the rock style of life at that time, there was no discipline.'

Taking the stage at just after three in the morning, Jimi began the Band of Gypsys' set by struggling through an uninspired performance of 'Who Knows?'. Clearly in no fit state to perform, he received little musical support from Billy and Buddy. Instead of playing safe by continuing with a crowd pleaser, Jimi led the band into 'Earth Blues', a new song recorded only eight days previously and not released until the posthumous album *Rainbow Bridge* (1971). Yet again, the music fails to come together.

Jimi commented to the audience: 'That's what happens when Earth fucks with space – never forget that,' then sat down on the drum-riser, obviously upset. Totally taken aback, Buddy Miles tried to reassure the audience, but merely succeeded in stating the obvious: 'We're not quite getting it together.' As Buddy spoke, Jimi walked off the stage and retired to his dressing room. Head bowed and pained by stomach cramps, he was a distraught and confused man in need of comfort and encouragement. Manager Michael Jeffery grabbed the concert debacle as the ideal opportunity to sack Buddy Miles. The Madison Square Garden concert marked the end of the line for the Band of Gypsys – finished before they even had a record out.

Jeffery had previously phoned Noel Redding on New Year's day, discussing the idea of him and Mitch rejoining Jimi for a reunion tour of the Jimi Hendrix Experience. Jimi himself had thought about the reunion, and had even considered it backstage at the Fillmore East when still playing with the Band of Gypsys, but had said, 'With Mitch maybe, but not with Noel for sure.' Jimi liked to party and jam with Buddy Miles, but as a drummer Miles wasn't nearly as suited to Jimi's expansive style as Mitch Mitchell. After signing contracts, Jeffery organized an interview with *Rolling Stone* magazine at the beginning of February to grab some publicity for the forthcoming tour. A skilled manipulator of the press, Jeffery sat in with the Experience for the interview.

Jimi made light of his disturbing performance, and neatly avoided pointing his finger at anyone – perhaps this was not surprising, considering Michael Jeffery was sitting right beside him. 'I figure that Madison Square Garden was like the end of a big long fairy tale'. Jimi said in the interview. 'It's the best thing I could have possibly come up with. The band was out of sight as far as I was concerned.'

When John Burks, the interviewer, pressed him for an explanation of his own performance, Jimi said, 'I was very tired. Sometimes there's a lot of things that hit you at a very peculiar time, which is what happened to me at that peace rally, and here I am fighting the biggest war I've ever fought in my life – inside, you know? And like that wasn't the place to do it, so I just unmasked appearances.'

In the same interview, Jimi was asked about how he wrote songs. He replied, 'The music I might hear I can't get on the guitar. As a matter of fact, if you pick up your guitar and just try to play, it spoils the whole thing. I can't play the guitar that well to get all this music together!' Widely regarded as one of the world's greatest electric guitarists, Jimi's comment could be interpreted as false modesty were it not so genuine. It neatly illustrates how Jimi was looking beyond the guitar, and suggests that his desire was to be a musician instead of 'just' a guitarist. Jimi 's further remarks demonstrate this suggestion a bit better: 'I wish I could have learned to write for instruments. I'm going to get into that next, I guess.'

Was this wishful thinking on Jimi's part, or did it express a genuine desire to broaden his musical horizons? Probably a bit of both. One thing is certain, however; he would have had to organize his life a lot better if he were going to apply himself to some serious musical study. The construction of Electric Lady Studios in New York City promised to make Jimi's erratic recording sessions easier to plan, but now there were problems which required immediate attention. Michael Jeffery and Jimi had been funding the ever-escalating construction costs from concert fees and royalties. Jimi hadn't toured since June of the previous year, and the royalties were not nearly sufficient to cover the costs, so what could they do to save the project? Jeffery went into hustler mode, and came back from Warner Bros. with a loan that provided the money for the completion of Electric Lady.

### RAINBOW BRIDGE

Part of Jeffery's deal with Warner Bros. involved Warners acting as distributor for a counterculture film that Jeffery was involved with, initially called *Wave* but later renamed *Rainbow Bridge*. Jimi was to provide the music for the film, and Warners would release the soundtrack. For all Michael Jeffery's practical business sense, he was also very vain, and hated the thought of getting older. So, what better way to show what a young, hip and happenin' dude he was than get involved in a youth movie?

*Rainbow Bridge* was to be directed by Chuck Wein, who had previously worked with Andy Warhol's Factory, the intention being to make the counterculture's answer to *Easy Rider*. Wein's theory was that *Easy Rider* was successful because the film's opening credits were shot at the Hopi Burial Ground, a 'high-energy centre' which miraculously energized the viewer. So, *Rainbow Bridge* was to be shot at high-energy centres such as Maui in Hawaii. To illustrate different facets of the counterculture, the film would feature surfing, yoga and meditation, plus the inevitable 'sex, drugs and rock 'n' roll', with Jimi providing the rock 'n' roll. Although Jimi was already behind in his recording commitments, he badly needed the financing for Electric Lady.

Meanwhile, the Experience were due to start rehearsing for their forthcoming tour. Noel grew restless as he waited for rehearsals to start, and made several phone calls to see what was happening. Finally, Noel says he got a reply from Mitch's girlfriend, who

▼ LP, Reprise, USA, 1971.

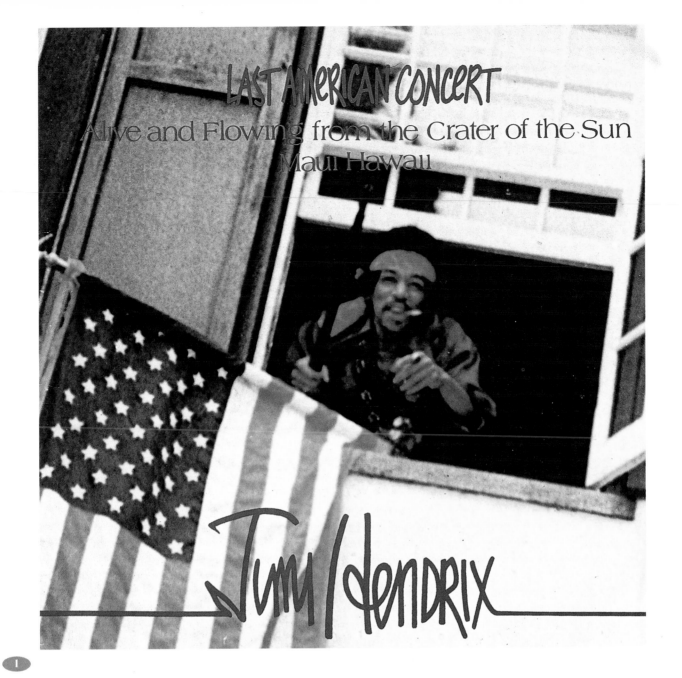

LAST AMERICAN CONCERT
Alive and Flowing from the Crater of the Sun
Maui Hawaii

Jimi Hendrix

**1**

1 LP, Bootleg, USA, 1977.
2 Video, Hendring, England, 1971.
3 LP, Bootleg, USA, 1971.

**2**    **3**

INCIDENT AT RAINBOW BRIDGE
MAUI, HAWAII
JIMI HENDRIX EXPERIENCE

▲ Singles, Reprise, USA, 1970. Jimi wasn't
happy with the mix, and the single was almost
immediately withdrawn upon its release,
making it a hard-to-find collectable nowadays.

told him they had already started rehearsing – with Billy Cox on bass!
After the show of unity for the *Rolling Stone* interview, Jimi and Mitch had
organized a clandestine meeting to discuss Noel. Jimi had already made up
his mind that he couldn't work with Noel again, but no-one was prepared
to phone Noel and tell him. Noel was understandably angered and hurt by
the rejection.

'It was always my plan to change the bass player even back in the days after
the Experience when there was no band,' Jimi later explained. 'Noel is
definitely and confidently out – Billy has a more solid style which suits me.
I'm not saying that anyone is better than the other – just that today I want a
more solid style. There's no telling how I feel tomorrow.'

Jimi was going through a rough time, and it wasn't just internal conflict
that was draining his creativity and energy – almost everyone around him was
making demands on him. Management, not one but two record companies,
girlfriends, fans, musicians, the press – everyone wanted a piece of Jimi
Hendrix. The promising start to the New Year with the Band of Gypsys had
ended in tatters, sending Jimi's musical career back into a freefall.

# 5

# THE CRY OF LOVE

"I WANT TO GET COLOUR INTO MUSIC.
I'D LIKE TO PLAY A NOTE AND HAVE IT
COME OUT A COLOUR."

*JIMI HENDRIX*

# PART I

## AMERICAN TOUR

The 'Cry Of Love' tour opened on 25 April 1970 with a sold-out show at the Forum in Los Angeles, performed for 20,000 enthusiastic fans. Beginning with 'Spanish Castle Magic', followed by the crowd favourite 'Foxy Lady', the new line-up quickly dispelled any doubts about their ability to play together, the rhythm section of Mitch's lively drumming and Billy's rock solid bass providing an ideal accompaniment for Jimi's guitar playing. Although there was no new record ready for release, Jimi introduced as-yet unreleased songs into the set as he had done towards the end of the Jimi Hendrix Experience period and with the Band Of Gypsys.

One of Jimi's new songs, 'Room Full Of Mirrors', had a strongly autobiographical lyric in which Jimi sang about breaking free from self-centredness: 'I used to live in a room full of mirrors/All I could see was me'. Played as a lengthy jam at the Royal Albert Hall in February of the previous year, the song had evolved into a more structured arrangement, with Jimi successfully juggling the multiple guitar parts that he used in the studio arrangement of the song without missing a beat. Tearing through the song with obvious relish, Jimi changed the mood by going straight into a Spanish-style improvisation as the prelude to 'Hey Baby (The Land Of The New Rising Sun)', the first concert performance of this song. Like 'Room Full Of Mirrors', 'Hey Baby' was another new song which alluded to new beginnings, and the music also suggested that Jimi was moving onto new ground. Just as 'Crosstown Traffic' from *Electric Ladyland* had shown Jimi moving beyond the traditional confines of rock chord progressions, 'Hey Baby' begins with an unusual chord sequence which modulates through several different keys.

Yet, despite playing the excellent show, *Entertainment World's* Jim Bickhart described the band's performance as 'deadly dull'. He wasn't the only critic to knock Jimi in 1970 with unjustified comments. Some critics were all too quick to assume that the short-lived Gypsy Sun And Rainbows and Band Of Gypsys line-ups, plus the lack of a new record, meant that Jimi had lost his direction. Jimi had certainly been through a difficult year, but he was recovering, and many of the audience tapes from this tour show Jimi playing as well as ever.

The relaxed schedule of the 'Cry Of Love' tour meant that Jimi could work on his next album in between live dates. Jimi wanted his next release to be a double album, but found himself in conflict with Michael Jeffery, who didn't think a double album would sell as many copies as a single album. Perhaps he'd forgotten that the double LP *Electric Ladyland* had successfully reached the number-one spot in the American album charts in late 1968?

Jimi had suffered glandular problems before the start of the tour, and even although the tour was restricted almost entirely to weekend dates, he became ill again, necessitating the cancellation of three dates. Since Jimi had arrived in London in September 1966, his life had quickly built up into an almost constant blur of gigging, travelling to the next gig, recording in the studio and jamming with other musicians at every opportunity. On top of that, there was the constant demand from the press for interviews and photo calls. The lives of top rock musicians in the nineties are often highly organized,

1. Double LP, bootleg, USA, 1970. The first time an audience concert tape was used for a Hendrix bootleg release.

2. Three bootleg CDs, all with the Forum 1970 material.

3. LP, bootleg, USA, again with the Forum 1970 show.

◄ **Berkeley Community Theatre, Berkeley, California, USA.**
*30 May 1970, first show*

with specialists to take care of every aspect of their career and day-to-day needs, but back in the sixties and seventies things were a lot more disorganized. It's hardly surprising that the stress and strain eventually took their toll on Jimi's health.

## KEEP ON MOVING

After his rest, Jimi was recovered and keen to play again. He had a rare rehearsal with the band before the next two shows at Berkeley on 30 May. The short layoff and the rehearsal served the band well, the two Berkeley shows proving to be among the best of the tour. Carlos Santana recalls speaking to Jimi backstage at Berkeley: 'He was talking about a new direction. Our band was getting more and more popular. And I think he saw that, whatever we were looking for, he could fit in.... Jimi used congas at Woodstock too. He was getting into Gil Evans and Sun Ra. He was hungry for the same thing we're all hungry for: multiplicity, but still retaining your individuality.'

◄ **Spectacular shot from Temple University Stadium, Philadelphia, Pennsylvania, USA.**
*16 May 1970*

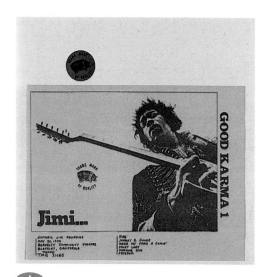

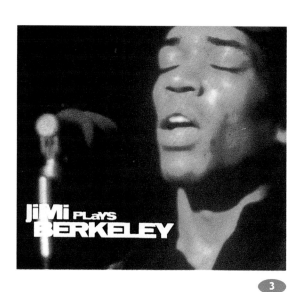

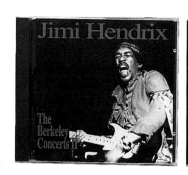

1. LP with Berkeley 1970 songs, bootleg, USA, early 1970s.

2. Video, Palace, England, 1971.

3. CD from video of Berkeley box.

4. LP, bootleg, USA, early 1970s.

5. Two bootleg CDs with Berkeley material.

6. Two cinema tickets, England, 1972.

7. Video, BMG, England, 1990 – re-release which comes with an extra Berkeley CD.

8. Poster included with the video release by Palace (see illustration 2 above).

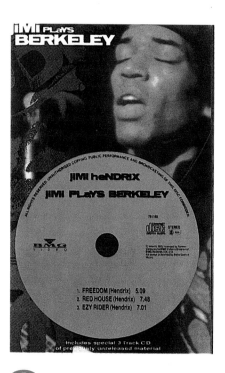

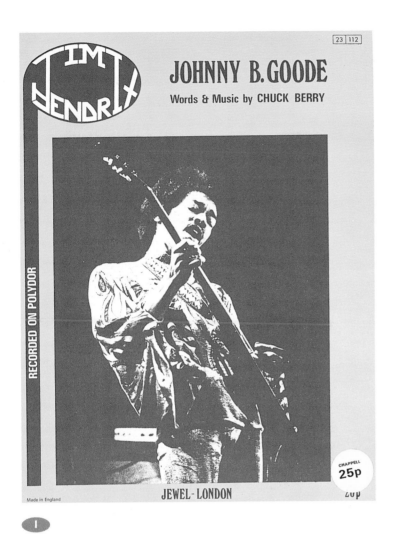

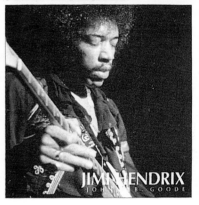

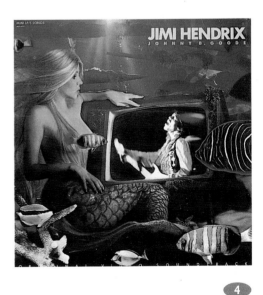

The Berkeley shows were captured on film after Jimi had expressed a wish to spend less time on the road and more time in the studio. Unfortunately, a film or video can never accurately capture the dynamics and spirituality of a musical performance, especially an artist with the depth and range of Jimi Hendrix. The subsequently released *Jimi Plays Berkeley* video also suffered from some poor editing, particularly in 'Hear My Train A Comin' (aka 'Getting My Heart Back Together Again'), released on *Rainbow Bridge* in 1971 (re-released in a different mix on *Blues* in 1994) – the video release fails to do justice to what was possibly Jimi's best performance of this haunting blues piece.

Other highlights of the Berkeley shows include an astounding version of Chuck Berry's classic 'Johnny B. Goode', later released on *Hendrix In The West* in 1972 – from start to finish, Jimi makes the song his own, jumping between the rhythm guitar part and lead guitar licks with remarkable fluidity. Although Jimi was at this stage concentrating more on his music and had less interest in the theatrics embellishing in his stage performances, he could still pull some tricks out of the hat when inspired, such as during this performance of 'Johnny B. Goode', when he played the guitar with his teeth.

Much as Jimi enjoyed playing live, he was eagerly awaiting the completion of Electric Lady Studios in New York City. Jimi's dream came true on 15

1  Sheet music, England.
2  Single, Polydor, Japan, 1972.
3  CD, EMI/Capitol, Australia, 1991.
4  Mini-LP, Capitol, USA, 1986.

▲ Video, Virgin, England, 1985.

▶ Lovely photo taken at the Atlanta Pop Festival.

*4 July 1970*

June when he was able to record at Electric Lady Studio, with Steve Winwood joining him for the first recording session. Although the building was still not completely finished, Jimi was able to lay down several tracks in Studio A, the larger of the two studios in the complex. 'From the moment the machines were in there, he was banging at the door wanting to come in...,' said Eddie Kramer. 'I remember I'd have a session [with another artist] like maybe from one 'till six, six-thirty. And God, he never was early for sessions...' he was there at seven o' clock, ready... "Can I come in and sit down, is that all right?" So I said, 'Jimi, you own the place, what are you talking about?!" '

July was festival month, with Jimi and Co. booked as headliners for several major outdoor festivals, starting with the three-day Atlanta Pop Festival on 4 July. Backstage, Jimi enjoyed a jam with Randy California in the dressing room before taking the stage. Opening with a slightly untidy version of 'Fire', the band settled down to turn in a competent but unspectacular set. Jimi was fond of inserting musical quotations into songs and played the melody of the standard 'The Breeze And I' during 'Spanish Castle Magic'. The Spanish-flavoured intro which usually preceded 'Hey Baby (The Land Of The New Rising Sun)' was unexpectedly played as the introduction of 'Hey Joe', and 'Hey Baby' is played as an instrumental to close the set as the fireworks overhead signified the end of the festival. As at Berkeley, the band's performance was filmed and excerpts were later released as the *Jimi Hendrix At The Atlanta Pop Festival* video with the songs selected in their entirety. The concert was also included in an edited form on the *Stages* box set (1991) as *Atlanta 70*.

Jimi made another festival appearance at the New York Pop concert on 17 July. The atmosphere became sour as the festival was hijacked by a group of radicals, the Randall's Island Collective, who insisted that their supporters be given almost every job on the site, and then let the audience in for free. Backstage, bands' managers realised there was going to be no money to pay the artists and complained to the organizers, who in turn feared there would be a riot if bands pulled out.

Jimi was always sensitive to the surroundings in which he played, and the ugly atmosphere had a detrimental effect on his performance. Yet despite this

▲ ▶ *Stages* **box set with four CDs, Reprise, USA, 1991.**

and the almost customary equipment problems, Jimi nevertheless turned in a blistering version of 'Red House', later released on *The Jimi Hendrix Concerts* (1982). Just when Jimi seems to have reached the peak of his solo and was about to return to the mic to sing the next verse, he took it one step beyond, cramming in notes with an almost-frightening intensity, interspersed with random feedback squawks, manic slides on the fretboard and reckless vibrato arm abuse. After going out on a musical limb Jimi winds down to sing the next verse, perfectly in control, and the audience loudly applaud his extraordinary guitar work.

Shortly after the New York Pop festival, Jimi found himself back in Seattle. While in his home town for a concert at the Sicks Stadium on 26 July, Jimi was able to spend time with his family. Seattle still meant bad childhood memories for Jimi and the concert itself did not go well, with yet more equipment problems magnified by the venue, a cavernous baseball stadium. Jimi's brother Leon watched from the side of the stage, and later described his perceptions of Jimi's attitude to performing in his old home

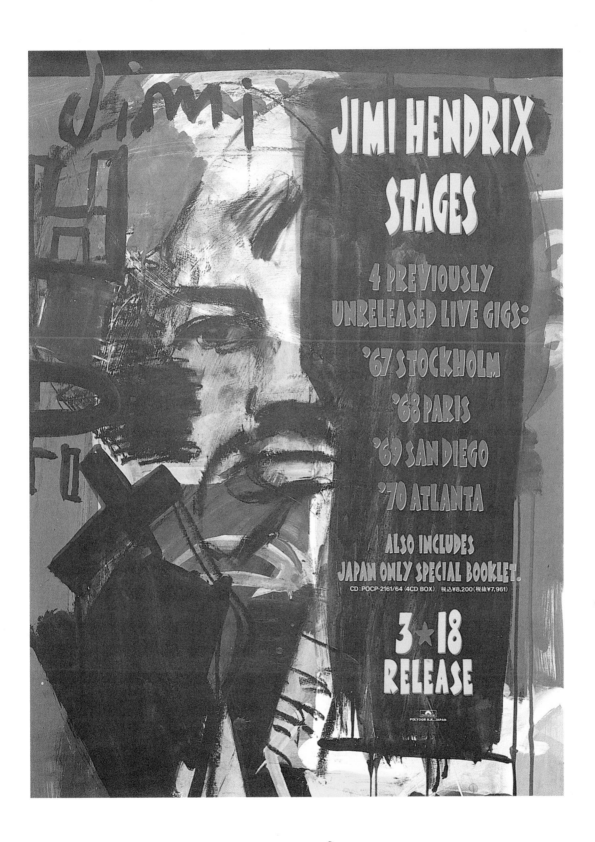

▲ Promotional poster, Polydor, Japan,
1992.

town: 'You could tell Jimi didn't really want to be up there. It was like he was looking at people, seeing all those who were against him.'

Freddie Mae Gautier of the Mae family that had helped bring up Jimi in his infant years also attended the show, saying, 'I was so upset, the acoustics were terrible, it was raining. This was Seattle's way of getting back at him.' The reviewer in the *Seattle Post Intelligencer* commented, 'To paraphrase W.C. Fields, "T'warn't a fit day for man nor beast".' The next day Jimi talked with Freddie about his problems and his life, including the idea of marriage. 'All my friends, they don't stay together. It's hard because I'm out on the road all the time.' Jimi valued his freedom, but as he later reflected, 'If I'm free it's because I'm always running.'

Much against his wishes, Jimi had to fly to Maui, Hawaii on 28 July to participate in Chuck Wein's film *Rainbow Bridge*. One of the organizers, Emilie Touraine, was interested in translating sound into colour, a concept Jimi had also expressed an interest in. 'I want to get colour into music, I'd like to play a note and have it come out a colour.' Jimi played two outdoor sets in front of around 800 people on 30 July. The shows were billed as the 'Rainbow Bridge Vibratory Color Sound Experiment', and Jimi's second set was particularly mellow and in tune with the beautiful surroundings. Both shows were filmed for *Rainbow Bridge*, but only a small amount of Jimi's performance was shown in the film, and most of the songs that were included were spoilt by very bad editing.

▼ **Electric Lady Studios card, 1972.**

And at no extra charge
Abe Jacob
Linda Sloman
Nigel Morgan
Shimon Ron
Ed Kramer . . . Dave Palmer . . . Ron Johnsen . . .
Ralph Moss . . . Buzz Richmond . . . Dick Shapiro
. . . Bernie Kirsh . . . Andy Edlen

ELECTRIC LADY INC.

electric lady studios
52 west 8 street
new york city ny 10011
212 777-0150

Jimi flew back to New York for more recording at Electric Lady Studios, which was officially opened on 26 August. He was justifiably pleased with Electric Lady, saying 'This is a different kind of studio. It's a very relaxing studio, and it doesn't have that typical studio atmosphere. There are lots of cushions and pillows, thick carpets, and soft lights. You can have any kind of light combination you like. I think this is very important. There are many capable engineers around now, the problem is the atmosphere thing. And we have the best equipment, too....'

The very next day, Jimi flew to London for a series of interviews before his next European tour. According to Juma Sultan, Jimi 'didn't have his heart into going to Europe. He wanted to continue [recording].' Even worse, unlike the US leg of the tour which had been carefully paced, the European dates had been arranged almost back to back, and the schedule was to take a terrible toll on Jimi's health.

▲ A rare quiet moment with some of Jimi's
relatives in Seattle, Washington.

*27 July 1970*

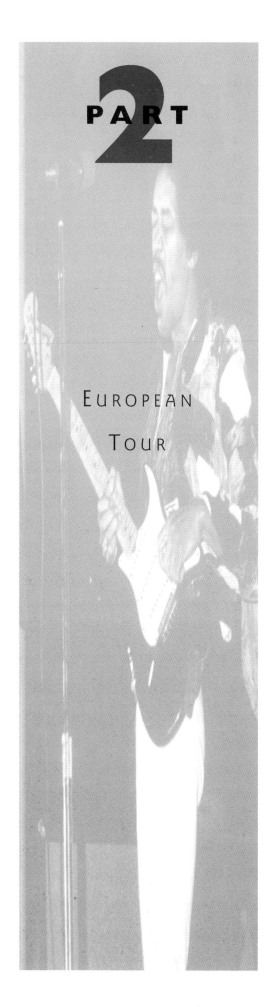

# PART 2

# EUROPEAN TOUR

The first stop on Jimi's final European tour was headlining the Isle of Wight festival on 30 August. Jimi had been looking forward to returning to England, the country which first acknowledged his talent. 'I really want to play England again. Do about eight cities or so. I'd like to go to Stonehenge, for the vibes. They're cooler heads in England when compared to America.' But as the hour approached, he grew increasingly uptight: 'I'm so very nervous about the Isle of Wight... I can't believe it. I really hate waiting around like this and that's what makes me so nervous. I think it would be better if I'd gone to the Isle of Wight and mingled, took a sleeping bag with me and mixed with the crowds, to identify with it all... but there are the usual problems. If I do things like that, people keep coming up to me saying "look, it's him".'

The last date of the American tour had been nearly a month before, and the band hadn't rehearsed since. Jimi had a cold, and since the band were going on last they didn't take the stage until a ludicrously late hour. Consequently, the Isle of Wight performance got off to an uneven start, and equipment problems such as amplifiers picking up radio transmissions spoilt the flow of the concert. Jimi hadn't performed in the UK for eighteen months, and most people were expecting to hear the 'blasts from the past', but Jimi had moved on since he last played in Britain, introducing 'Message To Love' with 'Y'all wanna hear those old songs, man? Damn, man, we're just tryin' to get some other things together.' Although the Isle of Wight performance was, and still is, widely regarded as poor, about half the set was actually very high quality.

Leaving the stage at around two-thirty in the morning, Jimi had no time for a proper rest. He had to pack his bags, travel by helicopter to the airport, catch a plane, check into another hotel, then meet the press and prepare for the next concert at the Gröna Lund amusement park in Stockholm. Just eighteen hours after leaving the stage at the Isle of Wight in England, Jimi was back onstage in another country, expected to weave some of his musical magic. In the big business rock world of the nineties, top rock artists are pampered as valuable commodities, but Jimi Hendrix couldn't even get a day off to recover from a major concert.... Thankfully, the next concert was also in Sweden, but then it was across the Baltic Sea to Århus in Denmark on 2 September.

## KING GUITAR

Anne Bjørndal interviewed Jimi before the concert in Århus, when Jimi still had not recovered from his cold: 'He was already talking about cancelling because he was not feeling well. He was uninterruptedly chatting, and saying "I don't think it's fair towards the audience as I don't feel up to it today...." He was also talking about harmony and peace of mind. Obviously that was the one thing he was looking for so badly... the music was his medium and he said "the guitar is something through which I speak and I sacrifice part of my soul every time I play." But what was quite something, which was to be my headline, was he said, "I don't think I will live to be twenty-eight". '

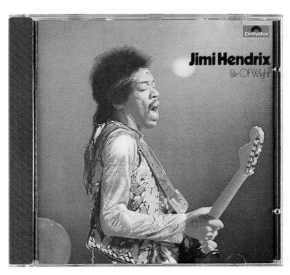

1 Promotional poster, Polydor.
Germany, 1971.

2 LP, Polydor, England, 1971.

3 CD, Polydor, England, 1988.

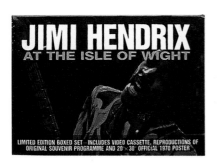

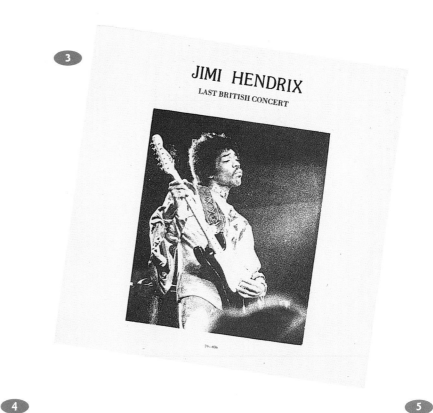

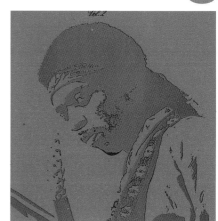

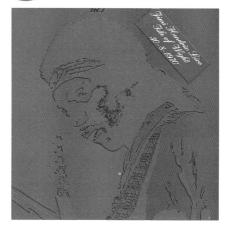

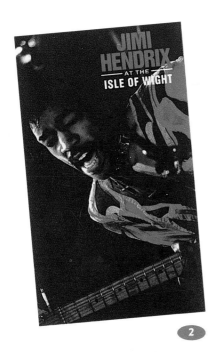

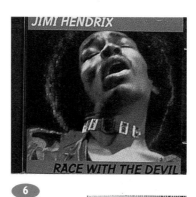

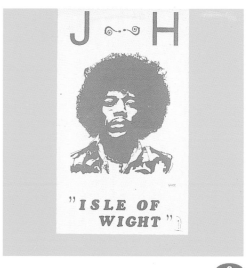

1 Limited-edition video box, BMG,
England, 1990.

2 Video, BMG, England, 1990.

3 LP, bootleg, USA, 1980.

4 LP, bootleg, England, 1970. Vol. 1
containing audience recordings from
the Isle of Wight show.

5 LP, bootleg, England, 1970. More of
the same on Vol. 2.

6 CD, bootleg, country unknown, 1994.

7 MC, bootleg, country unknown, 1970.

8 LP, bootleg, Holland, 1970.

◀ Jimi's concert in Copenhagen, Denmark, at the K. B. Hall, was his best during his last European tour.

*3 September 1970*

▼Tune-up time at Fehmarn.

*6 September 1970*

▲ Photocall (Jimi, Billy, Mitch) at the Isle of Fehmarn, Germany.

*6 September 1970*

▲ **(Left) Isle of Fehmarn photo on the cover of magazine *Pop* (Switzerland), 1972. (Right) Another nice photo taken at Fehmarn used by the magazine *Guitarist* (England), 1990.**

Jimi decided to play rather than to disappoint his fans, and the audience grew restless as they awaited show time. He flashed the peace sign to the audience as he took to the stage, leading the band into 'Freedom'. But after two more songs, 'Message To Love' and 'Hey Baby (The Land Of The New Rising Sun)', Jimi just couldn't play on, and he had to cut the concert short. Anne said that he looked 'exhausted and scared. That's how he appeared to me, scared, like a frightened child.' Jimi left in a taxi, saying, 'I just need a good night's sleep.'

Jimi also needed someone to talk to, and his friend Kirsten Nefer lent a sympathetic ear. The next day Kirsten took Jimi to her mother's house for some peace and quiet and Kirsten's mother cooked the family meal – a far cry from the rock 'n' roll circus that usually surrounded Jimi! After dinner, Kirsten and Jimi took a taxi to the K.B. Hallen, the venue for Jimi's concert that evening, but Jimi was growing increasingly apprehensive and didn't want to perform. Backstage, Kirsten tried to persuade Jimi to play, as the audience's growing impatience was clearly audible in the dressing room.

Describing her conversation with Jimi on the eve of this performance, Kirsten said: 'As I heard the foot stamping I told Jimi, "You better get dressed," but he wouldn't. Next thing, he took his acoustic guitar, sat down, and played. I've never heard anything like it. It was divine. That was what he wanted, just to sit there and play... then finally he said, "Okay, but I'll play for you and your family." Then he walked onstage and gave the best concert he had played in a very long time – just ask anyone who was there.'

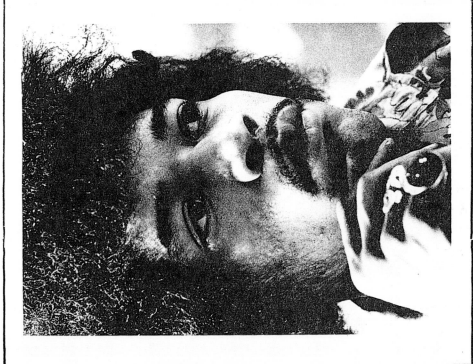

**LP, bootleg, USA, 1979 – containing part of
Jimi's Fehmarn concert.**

Jimi's friend from Los Angeles, Sharon Lawrence, was also at the show. 'Jimi looked the picture of health and played breathtakingly well. When he tired of the showmanship the audience so adored, he changed the pace and simply stood in place, a quiet, dynamic presence, gently bending with his instrument. The roller coaster was back on track.'

As ever, the media were as much interested in Jimi's personal life as in his music. The Danish newspaper *BT* printed a photo of Jimi and Kirsten Nefer, with the caption 'his Danish girlfriend.' *Se og Hǿr*, a 'gossip paper' according to Kirsten, went even further, announcing that Jimi and Kirsten were to be married: 'That thing about the about the engagement, they made that up themselves. "Wedding Bells" it states – that's too much!'

Although Jimi had achieved fame and fortune, the sense of insecurity which stemmed from his youth still had not left him. 'That's why he asked so many girls if they wanted to marry him,' explained Kirsten, 'That's what he wanted but he couldn't find out how to handle it, he didn't trust anybody.' Jimi's next performance was scheduled for 5 September at the Peace And Love Festival, Isle of Fehmarn. Jon Hiseman, the drummer of Colosseum, was also playing at the festival, and he remembered: 'We flew into Hamburg and were met by the representatives of the record companies. So there was Hendrix, Canned Heat and ourselves wondering what to do. We heard we had to get a train to the site, but nobody knew anything about reservations... there was no food or drink – the whole thing was a nightmare.'

Appalling weather pushed back Jimi's scheduled appearance by a whole day, and some of the audience greeted Jimi with boos when he appeared on 6 September. 'I don't give a fuck if you boo, as long as you boo in key,' replied Jimi. Opening the set with 'Killing Floor' taken at a more relaxed pace than the Monterey rendition, Jimi played a mixture of old and new songs. A slow and meditative 'Hey Baby (The Land Of The New Rising Sun)' was followed by a buoyant and up-beat 'Message To Love', but Jimi would still wail when the mood took him, taking a particularly aggressive unaccompanied solo after 'Purple Haze'.

Offstage, German bikers were causing havoc, robbing the box office at gunpoint and brandishing their weapons with frightening abandon. Jimi's road manager, Gerry Stickells, was attacked by the bikers and a stagehand was shot. As soon as the band finished their set they jumped into taxis and left the festival site, flying back to London. Further dates had been booked for the tour, but Billy Cox's mental health had deteriorated considerably after he had been given some acid earlier during the tour and he was no longer fit to perform. The remaining dates were cancelled.

On 11 September Jimi gave his last interview at the Cumberland Hotel after he had finished watching the Kenny Everett TV show. Keith Altham asked Jimi if he felt compelled to prove himself as 'King Guitar', the label many people attached to Jimi. 'I don't know. Well, I was just playing loud, that's the only difference [laughs]. No, I don't really let that bother me, 'cause they say a lot of things... King Guitar now, that's a bit heavy!'

As for his musical plans, Jimi was considering his options and keen not to rule anything out. 'I could feel, like, we could do tours with a small group again, you know, with another bass player. I probably get very wild, though, and wrapped up in the other scene again, you know, like the blue hair and so forth or the visuals.' But Jimi was also keen to explore new territory: 'I don't just plan to go out there with a ninety-piece orchestra and play two-and-a-half hours of classical music. I don't plan that at all. I plan for both of those thing(s) are [being] used, like rock and classic... without even knowing that it is rock and classic, with it being a whole new thing.'

On 15 September Jimi moved in with Monika Dannemann at the Hotel Samarkand. Jimi phoned Electric Lady to make arrangements for when he planned to return on 21 September, and also called his lawyer, Henry Steingarten, to gather papers together – he had decided not to renew his contract with Michael Jeffery. Later, Jimi phoned Chas Chandler with a view to working with him again; Chas said that Jimi planned to record at Olympic Sound Studios in London, where the Experience had worked in their early days. That evening, Jimi and Monika went to a party, then on to Ronnie Scott's club, where Jimi jammed with Eric Burdon and War – Jimi's last public performance.

Jimi spent the next day, 17 September, with Monika. They discussed art work for Jimi's next album – Jimi wanted Monika to paint the cover – then Monika took photos of Jimi in the hotel's garden, and they went shopping in Kensington and Chelsea. Stuck in a traffic jam in Marble Arch, they started talking to a man and two women in an adjacent car and joined them at their flat for a couple of hours. Jimi had arranged with Mitch to jam with Sly Stone and Ginger Baker at the Speakeasy club that evening, but he didn't turn up. Instead, Jimi and Monika returned to their hotel. Jimi had a bath, then Monika cooked a meal and they drank a bottle of wine together. Then Jimi wrote the lyrics for a song called 'The Story Of Life'.

After midnight, Monika drove Jimi to a flat in Great Cumberland Place for a dinner party attended by Devon Wilson and Alan Douglas, among others. Jimi drank some red wine, and Monika returned to pick him up. They returned to the Samarkand, arriving at about three am, and finally retired at around six a.m. Monika took one Vesparax sleeping tablet and fell asleep whilst Jimi was still talking.

According to Monika, she woke up at around ten o' clock in the morning and left the Samarkand around 10.15 to buy cigarettes. 'When I returned from getting the cigarettes, I went to Jimi, tiptoeing, because I didn't want to wake him u ... I knew he had a meeting with the record company that day, so I thought he has to have as much sleep as possible. So I went to see if he was awake... He was completely sleeping all right, there was nothing wrong with him.... At twelve o'clock he had the meeting. I sat down on one of the chairs and was thinking, "Shall I wake him or not?" And while I was trying to make up my mind, maybe three or four minutes, and watching him at the same time, all of a sudden I saw something came out of his mouth. So he

OBITUARY

## JIMI HENDRIX

### A key figure in the development of pop music

Jimi Hendrix, the pop musician, died in London yesterday, as reported elsewhere in this issue.

If Bob Dylan was the man who liberated pop music verbally, to the extent that after him it could deal with subjects other than teenage affection, then Jimi Hendrix was largely responsible for whatever musical metamorphosis it has undergone in the past three years.

Born in Seattle, Washington, he was part negro, part Cherokee Indian, part Mexican, and gave his date of birth as November 27, 1945. He left school early, picked up the guitar, and hitch-hiked around the southern States of America before arriving in New York, where he worked for a while with a vaudeville act before joining the Isley Brothers' backing band. He toured all over America with various singers, including Sam Cooke, Solomon Burke, Little Richard, and Ike and Tina Turner, until in August, 1966, he wound up in Greenwich Village, New York, playing with his own band for $15 a night. It was there that he was heard by Chas Chandler, former bass guitarist with the Animals, who became his manager and persuaded him to travel to England. Once in London he put together a trio with drummer Mitch Mitchell and bass guitarist Noel Redding, called the Jimi Hendrix Experience. The guitarist's wild clothes, long frizzy hair, and penchant for playing guitar solos with his teeth quickly made him a sensation.

His playing was rooted in the long-lined blues approach of B. B. King, but was brought up to date through the use of amplification as a musical device, and his solos were often composed of strings of feedback sound, looping above the free flowing bass and drums. The whole sound of the group, loose and improvisational and awesomely loud, was quite revolutionary and made an immediate impact on his guitar playing contemporaries.

As a singer and composer he was one of the first black musicians to come to terms with the electronic facilities offered by rock

music, and his songs and voice, influenced considerably by Dylan, created perhaps the first successful fusion of blues and white pop.

After his phenomenal success in Britain he returned to America, where he was banned from a concert tour by the Daughters of the American Revolution, who considered his onstage physical contortions obscene. That served only to increase interest in him and he rapidly became one of the world's top rock attractions. Then, at the beginning of 1969 at the height of his fame, he disappeared and spent more than a year in virtual seclusion, playing at home with a few friends. Early in 1970 he unveiled a new trio, the Band of Gipsies, and returned to Britain last month to play a rather unsatisfactory set at the Isle of Wight festival. In his last interview he was quoted as saying that he'd reached the end of the road with the trio format, and was planning to form a big band.

In direct contrast to the violence and seeming anarchy of his music, Hendrix was a gentle, peaceful man whose only real concern was music. His final public appearance was when he sat in with War, an American band, at Ronnie Scott's club in London last Wednesday, and it was typical of the man that it was he who felt honoured by being allowed to play.

▲ *The Times* (England), 19 September 1970.

## Complications, Not Drugs, Killed Jimi, Coroner Says

### By HENRY MAULE
Staff Correspondent of THE NEWS

London, Sept. 28—The last hours of Jimi Hendrix, the American rock star who died here 10 days ago, were described today by his weeping, blonde girl friend, with whom he was staying at the time of his death.

After listening to evidence given by the girl, Monika Dannemann, 23, and others, Westminster Coroner Gavin Thurston recorded an "open verdict" as to the singer's death. Although Hendrix, 24, had taken 18 times the normal dose of sleeping tablets, Thurston said there was not enough evidence to show there was a deliberate attempt at suicide.

Medical evidence revealed that Hendrix died through inhaling vomit due to barbiturate intoxication and that there was no evidence that he was addicted to drugs. Earlier, it had been speculated that Hendrix died of a drug overdose.

Miss Dannemann, a West German former ice skating star from Duesseldorf, said Hendrix spent his last three days and nights in her basement apartment in Lansdown Crescent, Notting Hill. On the last night, she said, she cooked dinner and they shared a bottle of white wine. She said he appeared very happy. Then, she said, he washed his hair, had a bath, and they talked and listened to music until about 1:45.

"He told me he had to go to some people's flat—they were not his friends and he did not like them," she continued. "He told me he did not want me to go with him, so I dropped him off and picked him up an hour later. He said he took some cannabis (marijuana) in that flat.

### Takes Sleeping Tablets

"When we got home, I made him a fish sandwich and took a sleeping tablet. The last time we were talking was about 7 a.m." With tears running down her face, Miss Dannemann, dressed in black, told how she found Hendrix still asleep about 10 a.m. when she awoke and went out for cigarets.

When she returned, she said he was still sleeping, but had been sick. She checked his pulse with hers and it seemed normal.

Then she discovered nine of her sleeping tablets missing, she said, and called an ambulance. She said she had never known him to take hard drugs, although he had told her he had tried them for the experience.

A Home Office pathologist, Prof. Donald Teare, said the normal dose of the type of tablet Hendrix had taken was half a tablet. A postmortem revealed no signs of drug addiction, such as needle marks, and although there were 1.3 milligrams of barbiturate in his blood, this was not a large enough dose to be fatal without the complication of vomit inhalation.

▲ *Daily News* (USA), 29 September 1970.

▲ *Disc and Music Echo* (England), 26 September 1970.

▼ *Rolling Stone* (USA), 15 October 1970 – note the year of birth incorrectly given as 1945.

wasn't sick when I came back. What I noticed when I left the flat [Hotel Samarkand] was that he was sleeping on one side and when I came back he had changed himself on the other side. He was still quite all right.

'So when I saw he was sick, I tried immediately to wake him up and I just couldn't wake him up. And I tried all different ways, shaking and everything and I just couldn't. So, not to forget he was a star, I thought I'd better call quickly his doctor. I knew the name of Jimi's doctor in London, but I only knew the name, Roberts[on], I didn't know the telephone number. I looked up the name and there were so many "Roberts[on]s", that I thought "forget that". I called up somebody I knew to ask her about a good doctor because I thought I needed a doctor and not a hospital. She wasn't there, but funnily enough, which I didn't know, she was staying with Eric Burdon.... When I reached her, I asked her if she knew the number, because she also knew Jimi or if she knew somebody else who was good as a doctor. She said, "No", so I said, "Well, I'll call an ambulance quick." '

An ambulance was called at 11.18 and arrived at 11.27. According to Monika, the ambulance men 'checked his heart, his pulse, his breathing and said it's all right, it's fine, nothing to worry about, especially as he'd only taken them [the sleeping pills] at the most three hours ago.' Jimi was taken to St Mary Abbots Hospital. 'Just as we entered the entrance to the hospital, the ambulance men started to move fast and put an oxygen mask on Jimi. So I knew there was something wrong there.' Monika phoned Eric Burdon and Jimi's road manager, Gerry Stickells, to ask them to come to the hospital, which they did. Monika waited for news of Jimi, then 'About ten minutes later [the nurse] came back and told me that he had died.' Jimi passed away on the 18th of September at the age of twenty-seven – just over a month before his twenty-eighth birthday.

### STONE FREE

Dr Martin Seifert, the medical registrar, said that Jimi was taken into Casualty. 'As a matter of routine when somebody is brought in dead or dying, they would call the medical registrar.... They had a monitor on him, and as far as I remember that monitor was "flat", showing that he wasn't alive. But just as a matter of routine [we] pounded away at the chest, trying to revive him.' At the inquest on 28 September, Professor Robert Donald Teare stated, 'There were no stigmata of drug addiction, once these marks are there they never go. In this case there were no marks at all,' giving the cause of death as 'inhalation of vomit due to barbiturate intoxication.'

Conflicting accounts of what exactly happened on the morning of 18 September 1970 led to a request in 1991 for the reopening of the investigation into the circumstances surrounding Jimi's death, but Scotland Yard denied there was to be a new investigation. In 1994, a request was made for a second inquest to be undertaken, but a spokesman commented that 'The Attorney General has concluded in the light of all the evidence that there is not an appropriate case for the granting of consent.' Monika Danneman recounted her version of events in her book *The Inner World of Jimi Hendrix* (1995). She was subsequently taken to

DECEMBER 1970/50¢

CIRCUS

HENDRIX-PEACE

JIMI HENDRIX
1942-1970

► *Circus* (USA),
December 1970.

court by Kathy Etchingham over some implied allegations in the text (Etchingham was
not actually named in the text), and was found guilty of contempt of court on 3 April
1996. Although she intended to appeal against the decision, she was found dead two
days later at her home in Seaford, England. The coroner recorded a verdict of suicide –
a tragic end for a woman who had devoted 26 years of her life to Jimi's memory.

Jimi had taken nine sleeping tablets – Monika said she had taken one, so the coroner
concluded that Jimi had taken nine times the normal dose. However, Jimi had said to
Monika that he needed a good night's sleep, so he probably took more of the tablets
thinking that these would help him sleep better. Professor Teare opined that nine Vesparax
sleeping tablets were not a fatal dose, and Jimi had only drunk the equivalent of four pints
of beer. However, the tablets and alcohol together had multiplied the effects to a fatal
degree. Although it was considered as a remote possibility, there was no evidence of any
intention on Jimi's part to commit suicide, and an open verdict was recorded.

After the news of his death hit the headlines, tributes to Jimi poured in from
throughout the world. Musicians, journalists, friends, fans – everybody who had known
Jimi was touched by his death. Jimi's body was flown to Seattle for his funeral, which
was attended by his close family and many musician friends. His body was finally laid to
rest at Greenwood Cemetery, Renton on 1 October 1970.

" Music is religion for me.
There will be music
in the hereafter, too.... "
– *Jimi Hendrix*

# 6

# THE POSTHUMOUS YEARS

"IT'S FUNNY THE WAY MOST PEOPLE LOVE THE DEAD.

ONCE YOU ARE DEAD YOU ARE MADE FOR LIFE.

YOU HAVE TO DIE BEFORE THEY THINK YOU ARE WORTH ANYTHING."

JIMI HENDRIX

Pass it on
LONDONDERRY HOTEL
PARK LANE LONDON W1
Telephone 01-493 7292
Telex 263292
Cables Landhotel London W1

(1.)

I aint always done right.
That don't mean you can always
Keep doing wrong pass it on —
        Pass it on —

I climbed mountains and
Mountains fell on me
But that don't mean I'm as
weak as I use to be
        Pass it on Pass it on.

I blew Dreams through a
Pipe of Steam ... But That
don't mean I'm a drag machine P.I.O
ect..

Pass it on
LONDONDERRY HOTEL
PARK LANE LONDON W1
Telephone 01-493 7292
Telex 263292
Cables Landhotel London W1

(2.)

the world is trembling
breaking) shakeing Heavy
Love making --- the Stage is
cleared for the Stars ...the
and the
GODS ... pass it on, pass it on
Angels come to come and came
and now they're trying
to be gone .... Pass it on ...Pass it
                                on
GOD help the Understanding
of love and sweat...
● Day and Night ....
rejoice and regret ... pass it on —

◀▼ **Jimi's handwritten lyrics for the song 'Pass It On' (later renamed 'Straight Ahead').**
*London, March 1970*

I stand up next to
a mountain and
chop it down with
the ledge of my hand...

I'm a Voodoo Chile...

Jimi Hendrix only released five official albums during his lifetime (and one of those was a compilation) but several hundred releases, both official and unofficial, have been released since his death. Less than a dozen accurately represent Jimi's art.

At the time of his death, Jimi had been working on a proposed double album. Initially called *The First Rays Of The New Rising Sun* in January 1969, by late June 1969 he had changed the title to *Shine On Earth, Shine On*, and then in early September 1970, Jimi was calling the album *Horizon*. Two posthumous releases, *The Cry Of Love* (1971) and *Rainbow Bridge* (1971) contained several songs which Jimi intended to release on this album, but whether Jimi himself regarded these songs as 'finished' and ready for release is impossible to determine.

## MR BUSINESSMAN

The legal arguments surrounding Jimi's financial affairs and the rights to his music have continued since the day he died. Jimi had made at least one will but hadn't signed it and his father Al Hendrix was named as the sole beneficiary of Jimi's estate. Press reports at the time suggested Al would inherit $500,000 – a small amount considering Jimi's considerable earnings. But when Al made inquiries, he was told there was only around $20,000 in the accounts. Al grew suspicious and hired the legal services of Leo Branton, a shrewd lawyer who had previously worked for Miles Davis and black militant activist Angela Davis, to investigate Jimi's complex business affairs. Jimi always had a cavalier attitude to money – 'I don't have no value on money at all' – and when he needed something Michael Jeffery would simply give him cash or instruct the office to take care of it.

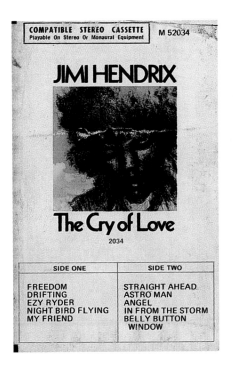

COMPATIBLE STEREO CASSETTE
Playable On Stereo Or Monaural Equipment    M 52034

JIMI HENDRIX

The Cry of Love

2034

| SIDE ONE | SIDE TWO |
|----------|----------|
| FREEDOM | STRAIGHT AHEAD |
| DRIFTING | ASTRO MAN |
| EZY RYDER | ANGEL |
| NIGHT BIRD FLYING | IN FROM THE STORM |
| MY FRIEND | BELLY BUTTON |
|  | WINDOW |

JIMI HENDRIX: best album ever

▲ *Disc and Music Echo*
(England), 20 March 1971.

# Hendrix LP, his last and his best

The last album JIMI HENDRIX made before his death, "The Cry Of Love" (Track 2408 101 £2.40), will be treated as more an epitaph than a new album. But as a new Hendrix album it is probably his best, although it doesn't contain his finest guitar playing. There are nine tracks and among the guesting musicians are Steve Winwood, Chris Wood and Buddy Miles, plus quite a few backing vocalists.

Side one starts with "Freedom," a strong soulful song, contrasted by the soft and slow "Driftin'," a floating melody with some weird sounding guitar, made even more liquid by Buzz Linhart's vibes. "Ezy Ryder" has the two Traffic men on vibes and starts off with a bit of a Traffic feel, but it becomes much more than that. It's really powerful with a lot of wailing guitar and phasing and it's one of the best tracks, pretty wild, with a fade out that briefly fades back. It's the only track Buddy Miles is on. Billy Cox is on the rest of the tracks with Mitch Mitchell on drums.

"Night Bird Flying" is a very funky track with some incredibly tense guitar. Side one ends in a light-hearted mood with "My Friend," party atmosphere in the background, just Hendrix playing and singing, bluesy, wordy, almost Dylan-ish, "Straight Ahead" starts the other side and the very poignant lyrics are printed on the back cover over a sunset. It's more typical Hendrix, driving along, and fades with some powerful wah-wah. "Astro Man" is about the heaviest track, with something more like the Hendrix guitar style that is best known, another fade out, fade in, fade out.

"Angel" comes as another complete contrast, ethereal, opening almost like Fleetwood Mac's "Albatross." There's delayed echo on Hendrix' voice, a beautiful track that builds up to a strange ending. Pity about the mushy drums.

"In From The Storm" is the hardest thing but even here he doesn't seem to be playing like he really could. If the lyrics of "Straight Ahead" mean something, then "Belly Button Window," the final track, will give you a spine chill. It's just Hendrix singing bluesy with double-tracked guitar — and the words are like he wrote them after he died—or before he was born.

Even if he wasn't in top guitar form, there are some of his best songs here, and they are the last we'll ever get.

Quality—outstanding; Value—fair.

1　MC, Reprise, USA, 1971.

2　*The Cry of Love* LP, Reprise, USA, 1971–
Track (England) used this same cover design.

▼ ▶ **Promotional book, in LP size, for the controversial *Crash Landing* and *Midnight Lightning* releases – Polydor, Germany, 1975.**

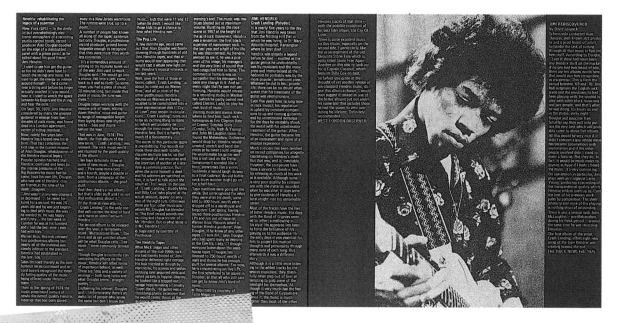

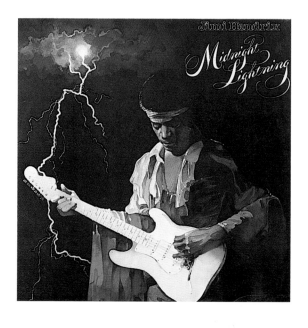

▶ (Top right) *Crash Landing* LP, Polydor, England, August 1975.

(Right) *Midnight Lightning* LP, Polydor, England, November 1975.

Branton made a deal with Michael Jeffery so that Jeffery bought Jimi's share in Electric Lady Studios and took on the remaining loan from Warner Bros. Branton then took Ed Chalpin to court on behalf of Track Records and Polydor – the ongoing dispute between the parties had meant Jimi's UK royalties had been withheld since 1968 – and Branton won the case.

Next, Branton attempted unsuccessfully to trace the funds of Yameta, an offshore company with which Jimi had signed an employment contract. An additional complication arose in 1973 when Michael Jeffery, who had helped set up Yameta was killed in a plane crash. Branton wasn't the only one with an interest in Yameta – since Yameta had controlled the finances of the Jimi Hendrix Experience, both Mitch Mitchell and Noel Redding were keen to see the mysterious dealings of the company unravelled especially since it was estimated that between $1 million and $5 million had disappeared into this company.

As Noel Redding explained, 'All the money from the early days went to this company in the Bahamas [Yameta], which was owned by another company called Caicos Trust, which was in care of the Bank of New Providence, in care of the Bank of Nova Scotia, in the care of whoever,' said Noel Redding. 'It's impossible to find out about these little offshore companies. They're just places where people send money, and then it disappears.'

Branton was told that the Yameta account was empty, and that to pursue the missing funds would be difficult, without any guarantee of success. However, Branton was successful elsewhere, and he managed to recover over $1 million for the Hendrix Estate, which helped to secure a comfortable settlement for Al Hendrix. Noel Redding and Mitch Mitchell were not so lucky. Jimi's former band mates had signed away their royalties in the seventies for cash payments when interest in Jimi Hendrix was still at only a modest level. Since then, sales have soared, and the royalties could have made both men extremely wealthy.

In 1974, Warner Bros. brought in producer Alan Douglas to work on Jimi's unfinished studio recordings. Alan replaced almost all of the original instruments on the tracks apart from Jimi's parts and brought in session musicians to put down backing tracks to create an album called *Crash Landing* (1975). This aroused a great deal of controversy – 'Is there no morality in rock and roll?' asked *Melody Maker* – but such was the interest in 'new' Jimi Hendrix material that the album was a commercial success, reaching number five in the US album charts. Alan was unrepentant in the face of criticism: '*Crash Landing* has sold two million albums around the world, okay? That's the response. I don't care what the purists say.'

*Crash Landing* was followed by *Midnight Lightning* (1975), another album in which the original backing tracks were replaced by session musicians. *Crash Landing* had received mixed reviews, whereas *Midnight Lightning* received almost uniformly bad reviews and was not nearly as commercially successful as *Crash Landing*. Even Alan acknowledged that he was 'stretching

▲ **Nice portrait of Jimi taken at the start of his career.**
*London, January 1967*

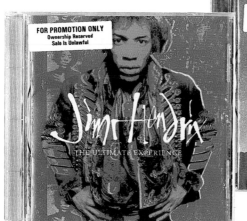

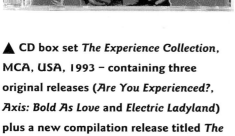

▲ **CD box set *The Experience Collection*, MCA, USA, 1993 – containing three original releases (*Are You Experienced?*, *Axis: Bold As Love* and *Electric Ladyland*) plus a new compilation release titled *The Ultimate Experience* – all with new artwork.**

for material,' and both *Crash Landing* and *Midnight Lighting* have since been deleted.

In 1983 a production company called Are You Experienced? Ltd. was formed to oversee Jimi Hendrix record releases and related projects, with Alan Douglas as the managing director. 'Jimi Hendrix's music keeps me going,' says Alan. 'I've recorded some great people in my life, but when I first heard Jimi, my past was over.'

In 1993 Al Hendrix fired Leo Branton and hired Seattle attorney Yale Lewis because of a 'wider questioning of the way his son's business affairs have been handled.' That same year, MCA bought the North American rights for the entire Hendrix catalogue for well over $30 million and released the 'greatest hits' album *The Ultimate Experience*. Al Hendrix was furious: 'If this sale can go ahead without my consent then I have been deceived... I'm so angry about this. Nobody ever informed me that the rights to my son's music were up for sale. If it's true, I think it's a total rip-off.' Al Hendrix started proceedings against Leo Branton and Alan Douglas for fraud and copyright infringement over their handling of the Jimi Hendrix back catalogue.

### CALLING LONG DISTANCE...

Also in 1993 – a busy year for Jimi Hendrix! – Are You Experienced? Ltd. oversaw the re-release of the first three Jimi Hendrix Experience albums. *Are You Experienced?*, *Axis: Bold As Love* and *Electric Ladyland* were released with new artwork and detailed sleeve notes, in effect repackaging Jimi Hendrix for a new generation of music fans. Alan Douglas believes that most of the record sales are due to 'to young kids, 19-year-olds, who are discovering his music for the first time.' Alan claimed that 'Market research last year [1992] indicated that 60 per cent of his audience is under twenty-one years old....' Sales of Jimi Hendrix records have significantly increased from approximately one million per year around 1988 to roughly three million per year in the first half of the nineties.

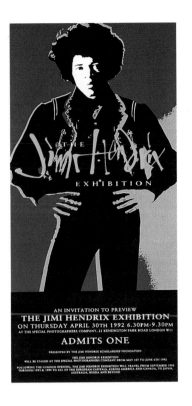

◀ **Two invitations to attend 'The Jimi Hendrix Exhibition' at London and New York galleries.**

*30 April 1992 and 7 April 1993 respectively*

At the other end of the spectrum, the international Jimi Hendrix magazine *UniVibes* has issued three limited-edition Jimi Hendrix CDs of previously unreleased material aimed at the dedicated Hendrix fan – *Calling Long Distance...* (1992), *Exp Over Sweden* (1994) and *Jimi In Denmark* (1995). Packaged with detailed sleeve notes and many previously unpublished photos, *Record Collector* magazine commented on *Jimi In Denmark* with: 'This is the wave of the future – committed fans issuing recordings of historical importance....'

The resurgence of interest in blues music in the late eighties and early nineties helped pave the way for *Blues* (1994). The blues had always been a big influence on Jimi's music, and *Blues* shows just how deep that influence was. *Rolling Stone* commented: 'It's hard to believe no one has ever assembled an album like *Blues* before... it's a great demonstration of Hendrix's guitar skills, but what sets this album apart is the way it illuminates the guitarist's debt to other bluesmen as well as his genius for pushing beyond those influences.'

As Al Hendrix remembered, 'I had listened to blues records ever since I was a kid. I had B.B. King and Muddy Waters records, they were forty-fives. Jimi used to listen to B.B. King and Muddy Waters, Chuck Berry and some others. I had a lot of records and he used to be playing them all the time and he'd plunk the guitar along with them.' Jimi also once said that, 'The first guitarist I was aware of was Muddy Waters. I heard one of his old records when I was a little boy and it scared me to death. Wow, what is that all about?'

*Blues* was followed by the the long-awaited release of Jimi's Woodstock performance. Although Jimi's Woodstock set had been previously available on bootleg, for many Hendrix fans the official release was long overdue. *Woodstock* (1994) was eventually released to coincide with the twenty-fifth anniversary of the Woodstock festival.

▲ **Poster announcing 'The Jimi Hendrix Exhibition' opening in London, 1992.**

▲ **Special A5 booklet promoting the Exhibition run in Stockholm, Sweden, in December 1992.**

1   **CD, Polydor, England, 1994.**

2   **Promotional CD containing two songs from *Blues* – Polydor, Brazil, 1994.**

3   **Box set containing the *Blues* CD, plus a 48-page photobook – UFO, England, 1994.**

4   **Front cover and label – CD, MCA, USA, 1994.**

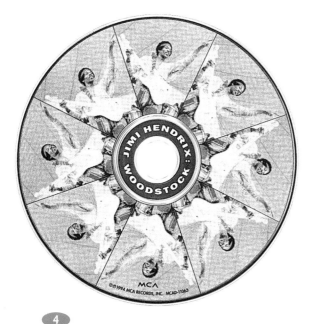

*Voodoo Soup* (1995) rekindled controversy over Alan Douglas' treatment of Jimi's recordings. A collection of songs Jimi was considering for inclusion on his next studio album, all but one of the tracks had been released before. On two of the tracks the drum parts were redone by Bruce Gary, the ex-drummer from US 'power pop' band the Knack, even although Mitch Mitchell was involved in the project. The Hendrix family expressed their disapproval of the project. As Jimi's step sister, Janie Hendrix, said, 'I don't really like it. It appears to be another overdubbing job similar to that of *Crash Landing* and *Midnight Lightning*. I don't think Jimi would like it either. The original band members were not used.' Janie also said that the family's goal in taking action against Branton and Douglas is to confirm the family's ownership of Jimi's legacy and to demonstrate that it is Jimi's music that accounts for his staying power, not the actions of Branton and Douglas.

The two parties settled out of court on 26 July 1995, resulting in Al Hendrix regaining control over his son's artistic legacy. Said Al after his victory: 'I am elated. Jimi would be happy to know we won this thing and got it all back.' Janie Hendrix commented that there would be no more tampering with the original tapes, although it still was not clear who would be in charge of future Jimi Hendrix releases.

In his music, Jimi Hendrix showed the boundless possibilities of the electric guitar, and he remains the single most innovative electric guitarist. He is a major influence on many top players, such as Joe Satriani, Steve Vai and the late Stevie Ray Vaughan, as well other black artists such as Lenny Kravitz and the artist formerly known as Prince. Jimi's musical influence goes way beyond electric guitarists and the sphere of rock music – from jazz to rap to funk, there are artists influenced by Jimi Hendrix. Even the classical music world felt his presence: the Kronos Quartet, Soldier String Quartet and Nigel Kennedy have all recorded Hendrix songs. The million-selling album *Stone Free: A Tribute To Jimi Hendrix* (Reprise, 1993) contained Hendrix covers by a wide range of artists, from the Cure and the Pretenders to Eric Clapton and Pat Metheny.

The vast range of artists who have performed Jimi Hendrix's songs demonstrates that his genius in music knows no boundaries, and that he will always be remembered and respected as a songwriter, as well as a remarkable guitarist. Interest in Jimi's music is greater than it ever was – a fitting tribute to a timeless artist.

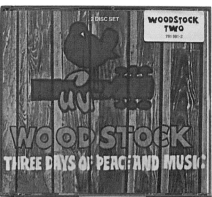

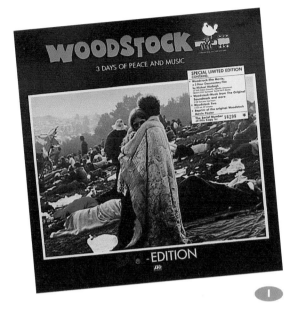

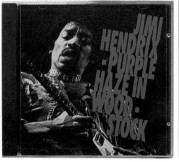

1 Box set, Atlantic, Germany, 1989.

2 Box set, UFO, England, 1994.

3 CD, Atlantic, Germany, 1989.

4 CD, Atlantic, Germany 1989.

5 Double CD, bootleg, Italy, 1989.

6 Double CD, bootleg, Italy 1990.

7 Video, BMG, England, 1992.

8 Three more CD bootlegs with
Woodstock recordings.

1    *Voodoo Soup* CD, Polydor, England, 1995.

2    Promotional CD, MCA, USA, 1995 – contains one song lifted from *Voodoo Soup*.

3    Jimi's music was interpreted by many other artists, such as The Gil Evans Orchestra.

4    CDs of various international artists doing Hendrix covers.

More artists including Hendrix covers/tributes on their CDs. Jimi's most-covered composition is 'Purple Haze' – up to now, some seventy-five different versions exist.

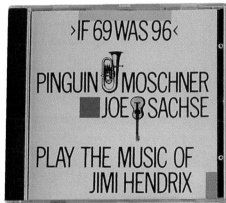

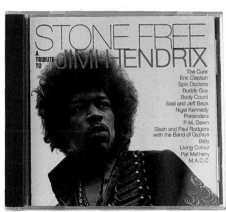

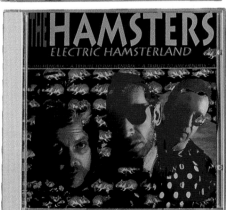

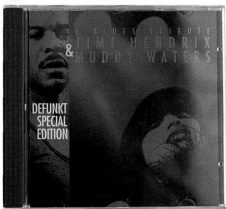

1  Promotional poster, Track, England, 1970.

2  Promotional poster, Polydor, Germany, 1970s.

3  Promotional poster, Polydor, Germany, 1970s.

▲ 'First Day Of Issue' envelope with Jimmy
[sic] Hendrix stamp from Grenada,
Grenadines, West Indies.

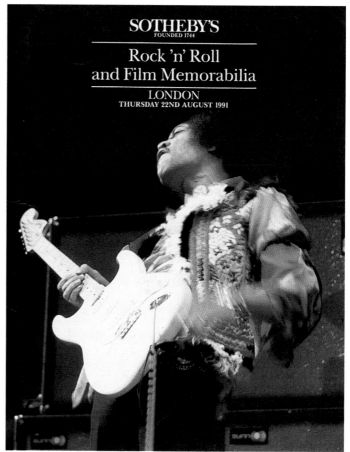

Hendrix memorabilia is 'big business' these days at various auction houses around the world – Christie's and Sotheby's being two well-known English ones. Jimi's address book is still gathering dust as it was withdrawn from a 1989 auction in London.

The best way to keep up-to-date with the latest Hendrix happenings, releases, etc. these days is via one of the many excellent fanzine publications:

1 *UniVibes* (Republic of Ireland).
2 *Jimi's Friends* (France).
3 *Jimpress* (England).

# DISCOGRAPHY

This discography is based on UK and US releases, and is arranged in chronological order by the original UK release date (or US date where there is no UK release). Catalogue numbers refer to record releases if there was no CD release; if released on CD, the CD catalogue number is given. A record and/or CD released in the UK and/or US could be available elsewhere, either as a separate release in another country or as an import.

The singles and albums listed under 'Jimi Hendrix Experience'

include the 'Band of Gypsys' and 'Gypsy Sun and Rainbows' releases as well as singles/albums released as 'Jimi Hendrix'.

The main sources for the discography are the book *Jimi Hendrix: Electric Gypsy* by Harry Shapiro and Caesar Glebbeek (William Heinemann, 1990) and *UniVibes*, the International Jimi Hendrix Magazine. It should be noted that the following discography only lists the more important releases – to print a complete discography would take up several hundred pages....

# SINGLES

THE JIMI HENDRIX EXPERIENCE

**'Hey Joe' b/w 'Stone Free'**
*UK*: Polydor 561329
*Released*: 16/12/66
*US*: not released

**'Purple Haze' b/w '51st Anniversary'**
*UK*: Track 604001
*Released*: 17/03/67
*US*: not released

**'Hey Joe' b/w '51st Anniversary'**
*UK*: not released
*US*: Reprise 0572,
*Released*: 01/05/67

**'The Wind Cries Mary'**
**b/w 'Highway Chile'**
*UK*: Track 604004
*Released*: 05/05/67
*US*: not released

**'Purple Haze'**
**b/w 'The Wind Cries Mary'**
*UK*: not released
*US*: Reprise 0597
*Released*: 19/06/67

**'The Burning Of The Midnight Lamp'**
**b/w 'The Stars That Play With**
**Laughing Sam's Dice'**
*UK*: Track 604007
*Released*: 19/08/67
*US*: not released

**'Foxy Lady' b/w 'Hey Joe'**
*UK*: not released
*US*: Reprise 0641
*Released*: 27/11/67

**'Up From The Skies'**
**b/w 'One Rainy Wish'**
*UK*: not released
*US*: Reprise 0665
*Released*: 26/02/68

**'All Along The Watchtower' b/w 'The**
**Burning Of The Midnight Lamp'**
*UK*: not released
*US*: Reprise 0767
*Released*: 02/09/68

**'All Along The Watchtower'**
**b/w 'Long Hot Summer Night'**
*UK*: Track 604025
*Released*: 18/10/68
*US*: not released

▼ **Tape box, Mayfair. This rare master tape**
**of 'The Stars That Play With Laughing Sam's**
**Dice' was found dusting away in a vault in**
**England in 1973.**

▶ 'Freedom' single, Polydor, Japan, 1971.

▲Promotional poster, Track, England, 1969.

▼ 'Let Me Light Your Fire' single, Track, England, November 1969.

'Crosstown Traffic' b/w 'Gypsy Eyes'
*UK*: Track 604029
*Released*: 04/04/69
*US*: Reprise 0792
*Released*: 18/11/68

'Stone Free' b/w 'If Six Was Nine'
*UK*: not released
*US*: Reprise 0853
*Released*: 15/09/69

'Fire' b/w 'The Burning Of The Midnight Lamp'
*UK*: Track 604033
*Released*: 14/11/69
*US*: not released

▼ 'Let Me Light Your Fire' single sleeve, Polydor, Germany, November 1969.

'Stepping Stone' b/w 'Izabella'
*UK*: not released
*US*: Reprise 0905
*Released*: 13/04/70

'Voodoo Child (slight return)'/'Hey Joe'/ 'All Along The Watchtower'
*UK*: Track 2095 001
*Released*: 23/10/70
*US*: not released

'Freedom' b/w 'Angel'
*UK*: not released
*US*: Reprise 1000
*Released*: 08/03/71
*JAPAN*: Polydor DP 1804
*Released*: 1971

'Dolly Dagger' b/w 'Star Spangled Banner'
*UK*: not released
*US*: Reprise 1044
*Released*: 10/71

'Gypsy Eyes'/'Remember'/'Purple Haze'/ 'Stone Free'
*UK*: Track 2094 010
*Released*: 10/71
*US*: not released

'Johnny B. Goode' b/w 'Little Wing'
*UK*: Polydor 2001-277
*Released*: 01/72
*US*: not released

▲Single. 'Gloria', Polydor, England,1978.

▲CD single, Polydor, Germany, 1988.

▲ Front cover of single, 'Waterfall' b/w '51st Anniversary', Barclay, France, 1972.

▶ Single, Polydor, Japan, 1978.

▼'The Collector's Edition', Polydor, Germany, 1978.

**'Waterfall'** (aka 'May This Be Love')
**b/w '51st Anniversary'**
*UK:* not released
*US:* not released
*FRANCE:* Barclay 61 389
*Released:* 1972

**'Hear My Train A' Comin' '**
**b/w 'Rock Me: Baby'**
*UK:* Reprise K 14286
*Released:* 08/73
*US:* not released

**'...And A Happy New Year'**
(promo single)
*UK:* not released
*US:* Reprise PRO 595
*Released:* 12/74

**'Gloria'** (4 track CD)
*UK:* not released
*US:* not released
*GERMANY:* Polydor 887 585-2
*Released:* 1988

**'Purple Haze'** (4 track CD)
*UK:* Polydor: PZCD 33
*Released:* 1988
*US:* not released

▲Single. 'Hear My Train A' Comin' b/w 'Rock Me Baby'. Reprise, England, 1973.

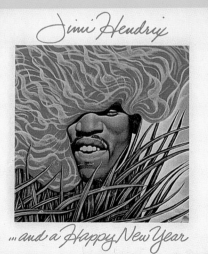

▲ Single of '...and a Happy New Year', Reprise, USA, 1974.

▶ Despite a very official-looking design, the picture disc (USA, late 1970s) reproduced here is actually a bootleg job.

▼CD single, 'Purple Haze', Polydor, England, 1988.

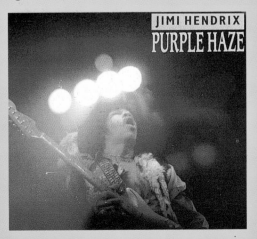

▲ **CD single. 'The Peel Sessions', Strange Fruit, England, 1988.**

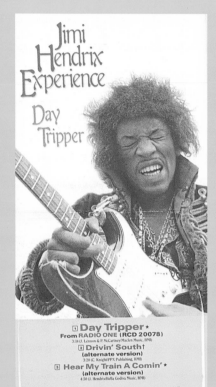

▲ **This 'Day Tripper' CD single (Rykodisc, USA) contains two outtakes from the BBC radio sessions not released on any other official release.**

▲ **CD single. 'Crosstown Traffic', re-release, Wrangler, 1990.**

**'The Peel Sessions: The Jimi Hendrix Experience'** (EP)
*UK:* Strange Fruit Records SFPSCDO65
*Released:* 1988
*US:* not released

**'Day Tripper'**
*UK:* not released
*US:* Rykodisc RCD31-008
*Released:* late 1988

**'Crosstown Traffic'** (4 track CD)
*UK:* Polydor PZCD 71
*Released:* 04/90
*US:* not released

**'Jimi Plays Berkeley'** (3 track CD single packaged with 'Jimi Plays Berkeley' video)
*UK:* BMG 791168
*Released:* 10/91
*US:* not released

**'All Along The Watchtower'**
(3 track CD)
*UK:* not released
*US:* not released
*FRANCE:* Polydor 879 583-2
*Released:* late 1991

**'The Wind Cries Mary'** (4 track CD)
*UK:* not released
*US:* not released
*GERMANY:* Polydor 863 917-2
*Released:* 02/11/92

► **This CD (Polydor, France 1991) offers an outtake of the song 'Come On' – only available in France, for some unknown reason.**

▼ **Attractive CD single cover from 1992 for a re-release of 'The Wind Cries Mary'.**

### WITH LONNIE YOUNGBLOOD

**'Go Go Shoes' b/w 'Go Go Place'**
*UK:* not released
*US:* Fairmount Records F-1002
*Released:* late 1963

**'Soul Food (That's A What I Like)'**
**b/w 'Goodbye, Bessie Mae'**
*UK:* not released
*US:* Fairmount Records F-1022
*Released:* early 1964

### WITH THE ISLEY BROTHERS

**'Testify (Part I)' b/w 'Testify (Part II)'**
*UK:* not released
*US:* T-Neck 45-501
Released: 06/64

**'The Last Girl'**
**b/w 'Looking For A Love'**
*UK:* Atlantic AT 4010
*Released:* 11/64
*US:* Atlantic 45-2263
*Released:* 11/64

**'Move Over And Let Me Dance' b/w**
**'Have You Ever Been Disappointed?'**
*UK:* not released
*US:* Atlantic 45-2303
*Released:* 09/65

### WITH ROSA LEE BROOKS

**'My Diary' b/w 'Utee'**
*UK:* not released
*US:* Revis Records 1031
*Released:* mid 1965

### WITH LITTLE RICHARD
### AND THE UPSETTERS

**'I Don't Know What You've Got But**
**It's Got Me Part I'**
**b/w 'I Don't Know What You've Got**
**But It's Got Me Part II'**
*UK:* Fontana TF 652

*Released:* early 66119
*US:* Vee Jay Records VJ-698
*Released:* 11/65

### WITH KING CURTIS

**'Help Me – Part I'**
**b/w 'Help Me – Part II'**
*UK:* not released
*US:* Atco Records 45-6402
*Released:* early 1966

**'Blast Off' b/w 'Pata Pata'**
*UK:* not released
*US:* Atlantic 45-2468
*Released:* Winter 1967

### WITH JAYNE MANSFIELD

**'As The Clouds Drift By' b/w 'Suey'**
*UK:* London HL 10147
*Released:* 21/07/67
*US:* not released

### WITH CURTIS KNIGHT
### AND THE SQUIRES

**'How Would You Feel?' b/w**
**'Welcome Home'**
*UK:* not released
*US:* RSVP 1120
*Released:* late 1965 or early 1966

**'Hornet's Nest'**
**b/w 'Knock Yourself Out'**
*UK:* not released
*US:* RSVP 1124
*Released:* early 1966

**'How Would You Feel?'**
**b/w 'You Don't Want Me'**
*UK:* London 5.620
*Released:* 11/08/67
and Track 604 009
*Released:* 17/08/67
*US:* not released

◄ **(Previous page) Jimi having fun during a**
**live recording of 'Top Gear' for BBC radio at**
**The Playhouse theatre, London WC2.**

*15 December 1967*

**'Hush Now' b/w 'Flashing'**
*UK:* London HL 10160
*Released:* 20/10/67
*US:* not released

**'The Ballad Of Jimi'**
**b/w 'Gloomy Monday'**
*UK:* London HLZ 10321
*Released:* 16/10/70
*US:* not released

**'The Ballad Of Jimi'** *(different version*
*from UK 16/10/70 release)*
**b/w 'Gloomy Monday'**
*UK:* not released
*US:* not released
*GERMANY:* Decca DL 25 430
*Released:* 10/70

**'No Such Animal Part 1'**
**b/w 'No Such Animal Part 2'**
*UK:* RCA 2033
*Released:* 02/71
*US:* Audio Fidelity Records AF 167
*Released:* 02/71
*GERMANY:* Bellaphon BF 18019
*Released:* 02/71

WITH ROBERT WYATT

**'Slow Walkin' Talk'**
*UK:* not released
*USA:* acetate single on The Mastering Lab
*Pressed:* late 1968

▲ Single, 'Hush Now'/'Flashing', London.

▼ One-off acetate single from 'The Mastering Lab', 1968 – Jimi plays bass on this Robert Wyatt demo. The song was re-released in 1992 on the CD *Calling Long Distance....*

▼ Single, 'The Ballad of Jimi', EMI, USA, 1967.

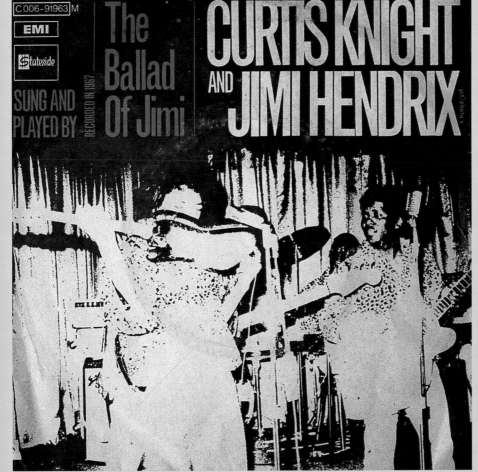

▲ CD single, 'No Such Animal, Part 1–2', Bellaphon, Germany.

▲ The German release of 'Rock 'n' Roll Band' (Buddah Records, 1969) was the only one that came in a picture sleeve.

WITH EIRE APPARENT

**'Rock 'n' Roll Band'**

**b/w 'Yes I Need Someone'**

*UK:* Buddah Records 201039

*Released:* 21/03/69

*US:* Buddah Records 2011-117

*Released:* early 1969

WITH LIGHTNIN' ROD

**'Doriella Du Fontaine'**

**b/w 'Doriella Du Fontaine'**

*UK:* Carrere Records 332

*Released:* 07/84?

*US:* Celluloid CART 232

*Released:* 07/84

WITH LOVE

**'The Everlasting First'**

**b/w 'Keep On Shining'**

*UK:* Harvest HAR 5030

*Released:* 11/70

*US:* Blue Thumb 7116

*Released:* 11/70?

▲ Single, Love, 'The Everlasting First', Holland, November 1970.

▲Two CD singles of 'Doriella du Fontaine' with Lightnin' Rod.

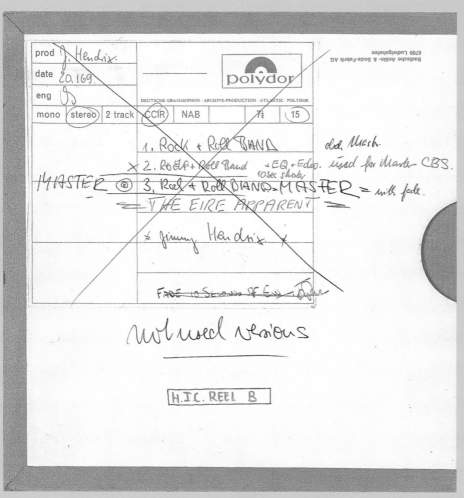

▲ Tape box, Polydor. Master mix of 'Rock 'n' Roll Band'.

▼ Maxi-single, 'Doriella du Fontaine', Lightnin' Rod, July 1984.

# ALBUMS

## THE JIMI HENDRIX EXPERIENCE

### Are You Experienced?
*UK:* Track 612 001
*Released:* 12/05/67
*US:* (with different track selection)
Reprise RS 6261
*Released:* 08/67

### Axis: Bold As Love
*UK:* Track 613003
*Released:* 01/12/67
*US:* Reprise RS 6281
*Released:* 01/68

### Electric Ladyland
*UK:* Track 613 008/9
*Released:* 25/10/68
*US:* Reprise 2RS 6307
*Released:* 10/68

### Electric Jimi Hendrix
*UK:* Track 2856 002
*Released:* end 68
*US:* not released

### Smash Hits
*UK:* Track 613004
*Released:* 04/68
*US:* Reprise MS 2025
*Released:* 07/69

### Band Of Gypsies
*UK:* Track 2406 002

*Released:* 12/06/70
*US:* Capitol STAO-472
*Released:* 04/70

### The Cry Of Love
*UK:* Track 2408 101
*Released:* 05/03/71
*US:* Reprise MS 2034
*Released:* 03/71

### Isle Of Wight
*UK:* Polydor 2302 016
*Released:* 11/71
*US:* not released

### Rainbow Bridge
*UK:* Reprise K44159
*Released:* 11/71
*US:* Reprise MS 2040
*Released:* 10/71

### Hendrix In The West
*UK:* Polydor 2302 018
*Released:* 01/72
*US:* Reprise MS 2049
*Released:* 02/72

### Experience
*UK:* Ember 5057
*Released:* 08/71
*US:* not released

### More Experience
*UK:* Ember NR 5061
*Released:* 03/72
*US:* not released

◀ **LP**, *Hendrix in the West*, **Reprise, USA, 1972.**

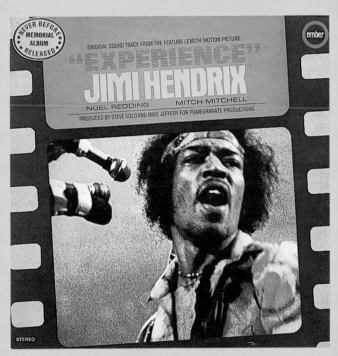

▲ **LP**, *"Experience"*, **Ember, England, 1971.**

◀ **LP**, *More "Experience"*, **Ember, England, 1972.**

▼ **Four** *"Experience"* **CDs.**

◀▼ **Few copies were pressed of the** *Electric Jimi Hendrix* **compilation LP (Track, England, 1968), resulting in over-the-top asking**

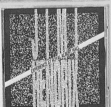

◀ Giant promotional poster (England 1973) showing Jimi stepping on a Wah-wah pedal at his Isle of Wight concert in 1970.

▼ Double LP, *Soundtrack Recordings From The Film Jimi Hendrix*, Reprise, USA, 1973.

▼ LP, *War Heroes*, Reprise, USA, 1972.

▼ LP, *Jimi Hendrix at His Best, Vol. 1*. Nice photo, shame about the recordings, which certainly aren't his best....

**Jimi Hendrix At His Best Volume 1**

*UK:* Saga 6313
*Released:* 06/72
*US:* not released

**Jimi Hendrix At His Best Volume 2**

*UK:* Saga 6314
*Released:* 06/72
*US:* not released

**Jimi Hendrix At His Best Volume 3**

*UK:* Saga 6315
*Released:* 06/72
*US:* not released

**War Heroes**

*UK:* Polydor 2302 020
*Released:* 01/10/72
*US:* Reprise MS 2103
*Released:* 12/72

**Sound Track Recordings From The Film Jimi Hendrix**

*UK:* Reprise K 64017
*Released:* 14/06/73
*US:* Reprise 2SR 6481
*Released:* 07/73

a film about
# JIMI HENDRIX x

*Featuring live performances from 1966 to 1970
including The Monterey, Isle of Wight and Woodstock Festivals,
The Marquee Club, Fillmore East and Berkeley.*

**Celebrating Warner Bros. 50th Anniversary** Ⓦ **A Warner Communications Company**
RELEASED BY COLUMBIA-WARNER DISTRIBUTORS LTD.

TECHNICOLOR    A JOE BOYD, JOHN HEAD, YES GARY WEIS PRODUCTION

Soundtrack available
on REPRISE 🅁
Record K 64017
Cassette K 464017
Stereo Cartridge K 864017

▲ **Promotional poster (England, 1973) for the successful Hendrix biopic.**

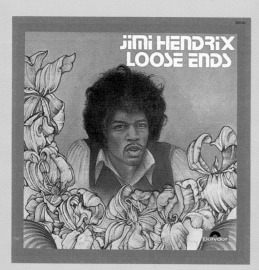

**Loose Ends**

*UK:* Polydor 2310 301

*Released:* 02/74

*US:* not released

**Crash Landing**

*UK:* Polydor 2310 398

*Released:* 08/75

*US:* Reprise MS 2204

*Released:* 03/75

**Midnight Lightning**

*UK:* Polydor 2310 415

*Released:* 11/75

*US:* Reprise MS 2229

*Released:* 11/75

**Rare Tracks**

*UK:* Polydor 2482 274

*Released:* 04/76

*US:* not released

**The Essential Jimi Hendrix**

*UK:* Polydor 2612 034

*Released:* 08/78

*US:* Reprise 2RS 2245

*Released:* 07/78

**The Essential Jimi Hendrix Volume Two**

*UK:* Polydor 2311 014

*Released:* 01/81

*US:* Reprise 2RS 2293

*Released:* 07/79

**High, Live 'N Dirty**

*UK:* not released

*US:* Nutmeg NUT-1001

*Released:* 11/78

▶The LP *High Live 'N' Dirty* (Nutmeg, USA, 1978) purported to be 'x-rated'.

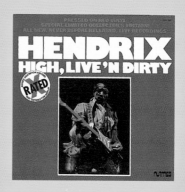

▲ Three different LP covers of *Loose Ends* – England (top); German (middle); France (bottom).

▶LP, *Rare Tracks*, Polydor, England, 1976. (Contains only one Jimi Hendrix track.).

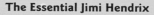

# RARE TRACKS

**JACK BRUCE · JIMI HENDRIX**
**SLY & THE FAMILY STONE**
**ALEX HARVEY & HIS SOUL BAND**
**FAIRPORT CONVENTION**
**NICKI HOPKINS · THE SOFT MACHINE**
**JOHN'S CHILDREN**
**KEVIN GODLEY · JETHRO TOE**
**THE HIGH NUMBERS**
**LINDA LEWIS · CREAM**
**STU BROWN & BLUESOLOGY**

◀ **Picture disc, *Woke Up This Morning And Found Myself Dead*, Red Lightnin', England, 1980.**

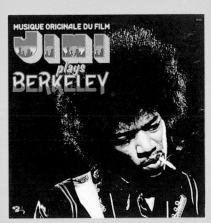

▼ **LP, *Nine to the Universe*, Reprise, USA, 1980.**

▲ **Despite its title, this LP is not the soundtrack of the Berkeley film.**

**Musique Originale Du Film**

**Jimi Plays Berkeley**

*UK:* not released

*US:* not released

*FRANCE:* Barclay 80.555

*Released:* mid 1970s

**Nine To The Universe**

*UK:* Polydor 2344 155

*Released:* 06/80

*US:* Reprise HS 2299

*Released:* 03/80

**Woke Up This Morning And Found Myself Dead**

*UK:* Red Lightnin' RLCD 0068

*Released:* 10/80

*US:* not released

**The Jimi Hendrix Concerts**

*UK:* CBS 88592

*Released:* 08/82

*US:* Reprise 2306-1

*Released:* 08/82

**The Singles Album**

*UK:* Polydor PODV 6

*Released:* 02/83

*US:* not released

**Kiss The Sky**

*UK:* Polydor 823 704-1

*Released:* 11/84

*US:* Reprise 25119

*Released:* 10/84

▲ **LP, *Message from Nine to the Universe*, WEA, Brazil, 1979. (The same LP as above, but with a different cover.)**

◀ **LP, *The Singles Album*, Polydor, England, 1983.**

▼ **Double LP, *The Jimi Hendrix Concerts*, CBS, England, 1982.**

▼ **LP size maxi-single with 2 songs from *The Jimi Hendrix Concerts* LP, CBS, England, 1982.**

▲ **LP, *Kiss the Sky*, Reprise, USA, 1984.**

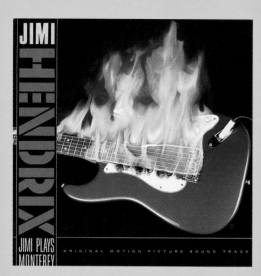

▲ LP, *Jimi Plays Monterey*, **Reprise, USA, 1986.**

▲ CD, *Radio One*, **Rykodisc, USA, 1988.**

▲ **CD box set,** *Live & Unreleased – The Radio Show*, **England, 1988.**

**Jimi Plays Monterey**
*UK:* not released
*US:* Reprise 25358-1
*Released:* 02/86

**Band Of Gypsys 2**
*UK:* not released
*US:* Capitol SJ-12416
*Released:* 10/86

**Experience**
*UK:* not released
*US:* not released
*GERMANY:* Galaxis CD 9006
*Released:* 1986

**Johnny B. Goode**
*UK:* Capitol/EMI FA 3160
*Released:* 1986
*US:* Capitol MLP 15022
*Released:* 06/86

**Live At Winterland**
*UK:* not released
*US:* Rykodisc RCD 20038
*Released:* 05/87

**Radio One**
*UK:* Castle Communications CCSCD 212
*Released:* early 1989
*US:* Rykodisc RCD 20078
*Released:* 11/88

**Live & Unreleased** (3 CDs)
*UK:* not released
*US:* not released
*FRANCE:* Castle Communications HBLP 100
*Released:* 20/11/89

**The Jimi Hendrix Concerts** (slightly different from UK 08/82 release of same name)
*UK:* not released
*FRANCE:* Castle Communications CCSCD 235
*Released:* end 1989
*US:* Reprise 9 2306-2
*Released:* 11/89

**Variations On A Theme: Red House**
*UK:* not released
*US:* Hal Leonard HL00660040
*Released:* 11/89

▲ **Cassette and book,** *Variations on a Theme: Red House.*

▼ **CD release with book version.**

**The Interview**

*UK:* CID Productions CID 006

*Released:* 1980s

*US:* Rhino Records RNDF 254

*Released:* 1980s

**Cornerstones 1967-1970**

*UK:* Polydor CD 847 231-2

*Released:* 22/10/90

*US:* not released

**Hendrix Speaks**

*UK:* not released

*US:* Rhino Records R-2 70771

*Released:* 30/10/90

**Lifelines: The Jimi Hendrix Story**

*(4 CDs)*

*UK:* not released

*US:* Reprise 9 26435-2

*Released:* 27/11/90

**Between The Lines** *(promo)*

*UK:* not released

*US:* Reprise PRO CD-4541

*Released:* 11/90

**Sessions** *(4 CDs)*

*UK:* not released

*US:* not released

*GERMANY:* Polydor 847 232-2

*Released:* 02/91

**Footlights** *(4 CDs)*

*UK:* not released

*US:* not released

*GERMANY:* Polydor 847 235-2

*Released:* 02/91

**Introspective**

*UK:* Baktabak CINT 5006

*Released:* Spring 1991

*US:* not released

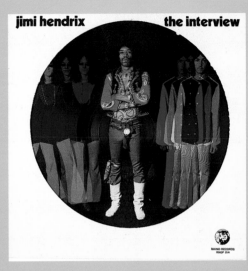

▲ Picture LP, *The Interview*.

▲ CD box set, *Sessions*, Polydor, England, 1991.

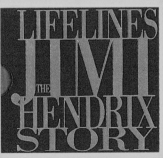

▲ Various Hendrix CDs, as follow (top left), *Cornerstones 1967–1970*, Polydor, 1990; (top right) *Hendrix Speaks*, Rhino Records, USA, 1990; box set, *Lifelines*, Reprise, USA, 1990; *Between the Lines* (Promotional release for *Lifelines* box set), Reprise, USA, 1990.

◀▲ The box set *Footlights* includes a new compilation CD of Jimi's Isle of Wight concert in 1970.

▲ ▶ Two *Interview* LPs (1969 and 1970 respectively).

▲ CD, *Calling Long Distance....*

**Jimi Hendrix 1970**
*UK:* Discussion Records Merman 1983 CD
*Released:* Summer 91
*US:* not released

**Stages '67 – '70** *(promo)*
*UK:* not released
*US:* Reprise PRO CD-5194
*Released:* 11/91

**Stages** *(4 CDs)*
*UK:* Polydor 511 763-2
*Released:* 02/92
*US:* Reprise 9 26732-2
*Released:* 14/11/91

**Live At Winterland + 3**
*UK:* not released
*US:* Rykodisc RCD 20038/3+
*Released:* 25/09/92

**Calling Long Distance...**
*UK:* not released
*US:* not released
*EIRE:* UniVibes UV-1001
*Released:* 02/11/92

**The Ultimate Experience**
*UK:* Polydor 517 235-2
*Released:* 02/11/92
*US:* not released

**Experience At The Royal Albert Hall**
*UK:* not released
*US:* not released
*JAPAN:* J!MCO Records JICK-89100
*Released:* mid 1993

**The Interview**
*UK:* CD Card CCD 4082
*Released:* early 1994
*US:* not released

▲ LP and cover, *Jimi Hendrix 1967.*

◀ CD, *Live At Winterland + 3,* Rykodisc, USA, 1992.

▼ CD, *Jimi Hendrix 1970,* front and back covers.

**EXP Over Sweden**
*UK:* not released
*US:* not released
*EIRE:* UniVibes UV-1002
*Released:* 25/01/94

**Blues**
*UK:* Polydor 521 037-2
*Released:* 18/04/94
*US:* MCA MCAD-11060
*Released:* 26/04/94

**Woodstock**
*UK:* Polydor 523 384-2
*Released:* 08/94
*US:* MCA MCAD-11063
*Released:* 02/08/94

**Jimi In Denmark**
*UK:* not released
*US:* not released
*EIRE:* UniVibes UV-1003
*Released:* 28/01/95

**Voodoo Soup**
*UK:* Polydor 527 520-2
*Released:* 04/95
*US:* MCAD-11236
*Released:* 11/04/95

JIMI HENDRIX
*"Stages '67 – '70" Sampler*

1 Hey Joe 4:11
2 Burning Of The Midnight Lamp 4:11
3 Purple Haze 5:23
4 The Wind Cries Mary 4:05
5 Red House 12:46
6 Voodoo Child (Slight Return) 10:16
7 Spanish Castle Magic 5:07
8 Hear My Train A Comin' 9:38

▲ **Promotional CD,** *Stages 67–70 Sampler*, **Reprise, USA.**

◀▼ **44-page A5 booklet that accompanies the** *Jimi in Denmark* **CD release – both UniVibes CDs offer un-released recordings aimed at the collectors still hungry for more Hendrix magic.**

▼▶ **(Right) 32-page A5 booklet that accompanies the** *EXP Over Sweden* **CD release (below).**

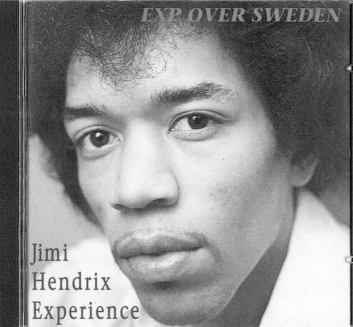

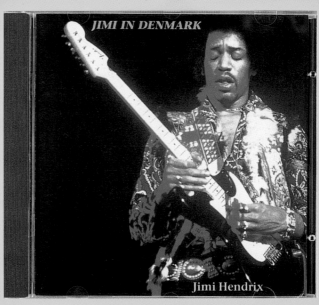

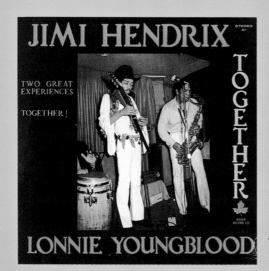

**WITH LONNIE YOUNGBLOOD**

**Two Great Experiences Together**

*UK:* not released

*US:* Maple Records LPM 6004

*Released:* 03/71

**Cherokee**

*UK and US:* not released

*ITALY:* Dog 'N' Roll DNR 001

*Released:* 1993

**Whipper**

*UK and US:* not released

*GERMANY:* Pilz 44 7430-2

*Released:* 1994

**The Legend**

*UK and US:* not released

*GERMANY:* Sm'art Art WZ 98015

*Released:* 1995

◀ **LP, Lonnie Youngblood, *Two Great Experiences Together*, Maple Record, USA.**

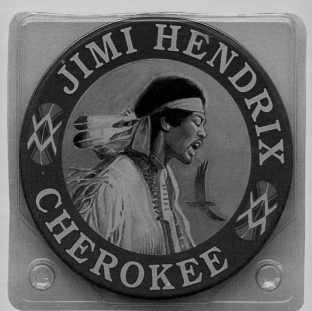

▲ ▼ ▶ **These three CD releases –** *Cherokee*, *The Legend* **and** *Whipper* **–
are not included for their musical contents, but only because they come
in tins. Whatever next?**

## WITH THE ISLEY BROTHERS

**In The Beginning**

*UK:* not released

*US:* T-Neck TNS 3007

*Released:* early 70s

*GERMANY:* Brunswick 2911 508

*Released:* early 1970s

## WITH CURTIS KNIGHT

**Get That Feeling**

*UK:* London SH 8349

*Released:* 12/67

*US:* Capitol ST 2856

*Released:* 12/67

**The Great Jimi Hendrix In New York**

*UK:* not released

*US:* not released

Holland: London 379 008

*Released:* 12/68

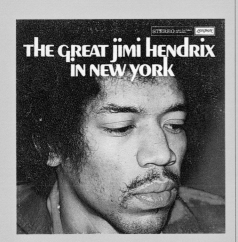

▲ LP box set, *The Great Jimi Hendrix in New York*, London, Holland, 1968.

**Flashing/Jimi Hendrix Plays Curtis Knight Sings**

*UK:* not released

*US:* Capitol ST 2894

*Released:* late 1968

**Early Jimi Hendrix**

*UK:* not released

*US:* not released

*HOLLAND:* Stateside 5C 054-91962

*Released:* early 1970s

**Early Jimi Hendrix Vol. II**

*UK:* not released

*US:* not released

*HOLLAND:* $tateside 5C 052-92031

*Released:* early 1970s

**What'd I Say**

*UK:* not released

*Released:* 07/72

*US:* Music For Pleasure MFP 5278

*Released:* 07/72

**In The Beginning**

*UK:* Ember NR 5068

*Released:* 1973

*US:* not released

**Looking Back With Jimi Hendrix**

*UK:* Ember EMB 3428

*Released:* 02/75

*US:* not released

**Last Night**

*UK:* not released

*US:* not released

*GERMANY:* Astan 201016

*Released:* 1981

▶ LP, *Last Night*, Astan, 1981. (Oops, somebody forgot to mention Knight on the record.)

◀ LP, *Early Jimi Hendrix Vol. II*, EMI.

▲ Two LPs, *In The Beginning – Jimi Hendrix and the Isley Brothers*, Polydor, Germany 1970s.

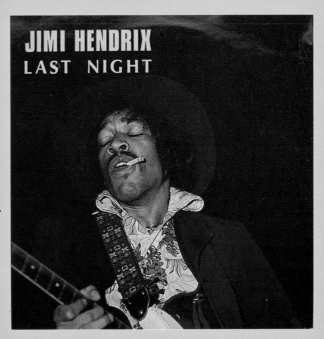

▲ LP, *McGough & McGear*, re-release from 1989, EMI. Jimi plays lead guitar on the tracks 'So Much' and 'Ex Art Student' – the original and the re-release (shown here) have both been deleted.

▶ (Above right) LP, *Sunrise*, Buddah Records, USA, May 1969. Jimi produced the first LP from Eire Apparent and also played on several of its songs.

▼ LP, *Stephen Stills*, Atlantic, USA, November 1970. During March 1970 Jimi laid down a few tracks with Stephen Stills – only one song, 'Old Times Good Times', has been released (on this LP) thus far.

WITH MCGOUGH & MCGEAR

**McGough & McGear**

*UK:* EMI Parlophone PCS 7047

*Released:* 10/04/68

*US:* not released

WITH EIRE APPARENT

**Sunrise**

*UK:* Buddah Records 203 021

*Released:* 05/69

*US:* Buddah Records BDS 5031

*Released:* 1969

WITH TIMOTHY LEARY

**You Can Be Anyone This Time Around**

*UK:* not released

*US:* Douglas 1

*Released:* 04/70

WITH STEPHEN STILLS

**Stephen Stills**

*UK:* Atlantic 2401 004

*Released:* 11/70

*US:* Atlantic SD 720

*Released:* 11/70

◀ LP, *Love*, Blue Thumb, USA, December 1970. Arthur Lee (founder of the group Love) and Jimi Hendrix go back a very long time – in 1970 the pair bumped into each other in London, resulting in Jimi doing a guest spot on the song 'The Everlasting First' (released on this LP and also as a single).

## WITH LOVE

**False Start**

UK: not released

US: Blue Thumb BTS 22

*Released:* 12/70

## CAT MOTHER AND THE ALL NIGHT NEWSBOYS

**The Street Giveth...and The Street Taketh Away**

UK: Polydor 184 300

*Released:* 06/69

US: Polydor 24-4001

*Released:* 06/69

## VARIOUS ARTISTS' COMPILATION ALBUMS

**Historical Performances Recorded At The Monterey International Pop Festival** *(includes four Hendrix tracks)*

UK: not released

US: Reprise MS 2029

*Released:* 09/70

**Woodstock**

*(includes three Hendrix tracks)*

UK: Atlantic K60001

*Released:* 06/70

US: Cotillion SD 3500

*Released:* 06/70

▲ LP, *Cat Mother and the All Night Newsboys*, Polydor, USA, 1970. Michael Jeffery also managed Cat Mother, so it comes perhaps as no surprise that Jimi Hendrix produced this LP. The results weren't all that impressive, though.

◀ LP, *You Can Be Anyone This Time Around*, USA, April 1970. Again, only one song, 'Live and Let Live', features Jimi on this release, but this time he plays bass.

▲ This CD, released by magazine *Rock Compact Disc*, contains two versions of 'Red House' – one by Jimi Hendrix (live from the Royal Albert Hall, 1969) and a cover by John Lee Hooker, recorded in 1989.

▲ LP, *The Best of Jimi Hendrix*, Polydor, Holland, 1970s.

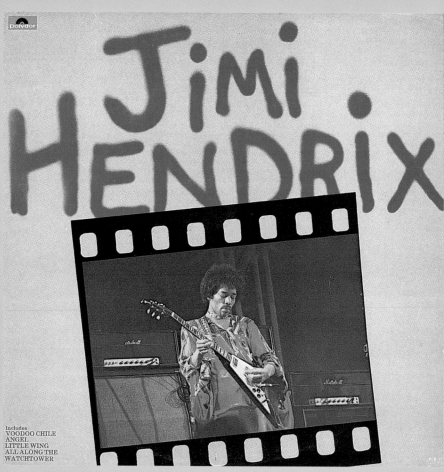

▲ LP, *Jimi Hendrix*, Polydor, England, 1975.

▲ LP, *Jimi Hendrix Vol 2*, Polydor, England, 1976.

**Woodstock Two**
*(includes three Hendrix tracks)*
*UK:* Atlantic K60002
*Released:* 04/71
*US:* Cotillion SD 2400
*Released:* 04/71

**The First Great Rock Festivals Of The Seventies: Isle Of Wight/Atlanta Pop Festival** *(includes three Hendrix tracks)*
*UK:* CBS 66311
*Released:* 10/71
*US:* Columbia G3X 30805
*Released:* 09/71

**RCD Classic Rock Collection Vol 1**
*(includes one Hendrix track)*
*UK:* Rock Compact Disc RCD 1
*Released:* 03/93
*US:* not released

**Live Forever: Sacred Sources 1**
*(includes three Hendrix tracks)*
*UK:* Polydor 521 321 2
*Released:* 11?/93
*US:* Guts & Grace/Cohiba 697 124 004-2
*Released:* 11/93

▼ ▶ **Many compilation releases continue to flood the market. This** *Legacy* **double LP (Polydor, Japan, late 70s – back and front covers shown here) is one of the better ones as far as design goes.**

柴のけむり／風の中のマリー／ヘイ・ジョー／賭博師サムのサイコロ／ハイウエイ・チャイル・ユー・シー・ミー／ファイアー／マニック・デプレッション／レッド・ハウス／ストーン・フリー／フォクシー・レディ／キャンド／クロス・タウン・トラフィック／静かな雨、静かな拳／ウォッチタワー／ラヴ・オア・コンフュージョン／エレクトリック・レディランマジック／明日まで待って／ソウル・パワー／恋のメッセージ／ジプシー・アイズ／真夜中のランプ／スパニッシュ・キャッスル・／チェンジズ

Jimi Hendrix
Legacy

▲ Flexi-single included with *Rolling Stone* (England), 13 September 1973.

▲ Flexi-single included with *Poster Press* (Germany), Summer 1974.

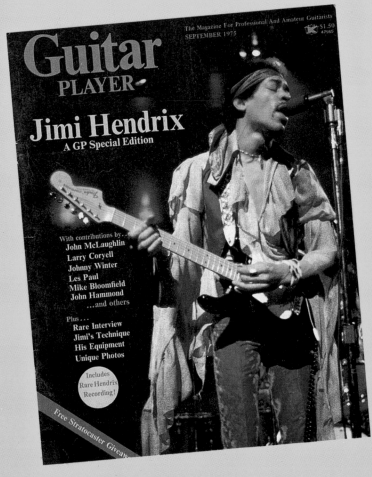

▲ ▶ *Guitar Player* (USA) magazine including flexi-single (right) September 1975.

MAXI SINGLE 2141 227

Polydor

## Special Version
## 33 rpm

# JIMI HENDRIX

# GLORIA
8:47
(NEVER RELEASED IN GERMANY)

# HEY JOE
3:22

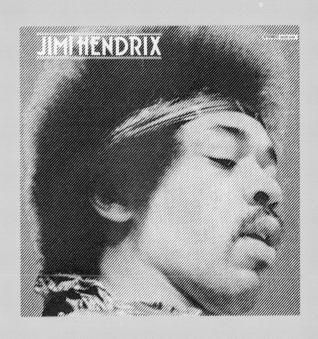

▲ ▶ This box set (Polydor, Germany, 1980) contains 12 LPs, a booklet (above right), a poster, and the 'Gloria' single (right) released in LP size. However, it's really only something for the completists, as it offers no new music.

Including
SUPER MAXI SINGLE
»GLORIA«
which has never been
released before
2625 038

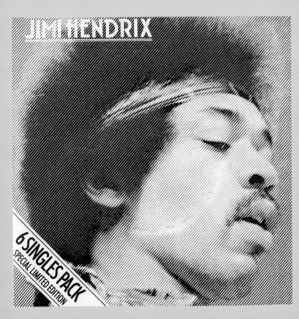

6 SINGLES PACK
SPECIAL LIMITED EDITION

▲ And yet another 'special limited edition' – this time a '6 singles pack' (Polydor, Germany, 1980).

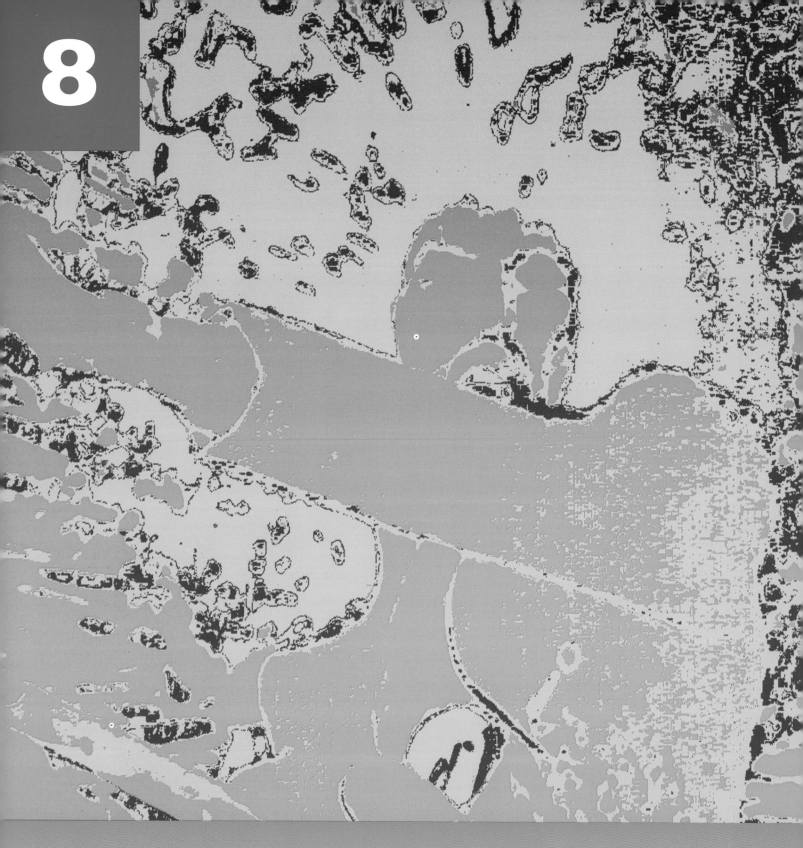

# 8

# BOOTLEGS

"SOME CAT WENT TO A PRIVATE PRACTICE [*sic*] SESSION

WITH A TINY TAPE RECORDER AND MADE A PIRATE LP.

THE QUALITY MUST BE TERRIBLE."

*JIMI HENDRIX*

The first rock bootleg record was pressed in 1969, a collection of unreleased Bob Dylan recordings called *Great White Wonder*. Despite changes in the law in both America and Europe to protect artists and record companies from unauthorised releases, the bootleg industry has continued to supply enthusiastic music fans with unofficial recordings of their favourite artists. Bootleg recordings are largely confined to rock acts, with little crossover into pop or soul; the most bootlegged artists are the 'big five' of Bob Dylan, the Beatles, Led Zeppelin, the Rolling Stones and Bruce Springsteen, with Jimi Hendrix not far behind.

## THE CONCEPT

Bootleg recordings are nearly always of material that has not been released officially, and they nearly always bear their own distinctive art work. Bootlegs differ from pirate or counterfeit albums, which are illegally manufactured to look and sound exactly like an official release. Although pirated albums and home taping are far bigger problems than bootlegs, the BPI (British Phonographic Industry) and record companies still strongly object to bootleg because the bootleggers do not pay monies to the record company or the artist. The counter-argument is that bootleg buyers generally own all the officially available recordings of an artist, and that the record company woul not have released the bootlegged material in the first place because it is of limited interest to the average fan of any particular artist. So, bootleggers would argue that they are supplying a niche market too small for the record company to cater for – the typical bootleg run is between 500 and 2,500 copies. Nevertheless, record companies still object to the commercial exploitation of something that 'belongs' to them.

Many artists also disapprove of bootlegging, and some take measures to beat the bootlegger. In order to minimize the commercial bootlegging of their shows, the Grateful Dead encourage fans to tape live gigs. The late Frank Zappa issued two *Beat The Boots* box sets (Rhino Records, 1991 anc 1992), comprising of counterfeits of existing Zappa bootlegs priced at a leve to undercut the bootleggers and to make money from the bootlegger's industry. Artists can hardly object to bootlegging on the grounds that they a losing royalties on something they never intended for release in the first plac but they have a valid point when they argue that control is being taken awa from them, and that someone is making money from their work.

Until the end of the 80s, bootlegs mainly appeared as LPs, but then they were replaced by CDs as the most common medium. In the late 80s and ear 90s, bootleggers exploited anomalies in European copyright laws to produce so-called 'protection gap' bootlegs – legitimate but unauthorized releases in the country of origin, which have questionable legality when exported. Italy is probably the most prolific country for producing unauthorized CDs, since Italian labels do not require authorization from an artist to release a live performance. Under Italian law, a live CD obtains legitimacy if it carries an SIAE stamp from the Italian body responsible for collecting royalties (the German equivalent is GEMA). For the first time in the history of bootlegging, CD producers were paying royalties on the product in order tc

This flyer
is for that
MAN who
walked into
A pad at Woodstock
raised his AXE
and talked
To the people
Around him,
And they talked
Together.

▲ *This Flyer* was the very first Hendrix bootleg (USA, April 1970 – based on Shokan house material from Autumn 1969, with Juma, Mike Ephron, etc.) to appear on the market. Twenty-six years later, you need a very large overdraft to keep afloat with the several hundreds of illegal releases!

get the SIAE stamp and expand into conventional retail outlets.

The export of these CDs from Italy to other countries with different copyright laws such as the UK has led to the occasional availability of 'grey area' CDs in regular high street record shops. Of course, such releases still remain unauthorized, but the legality or otherwise of these releases has yet to be proved. In 1995 the SIAE bowed to pressure from the major record companies and other interests to stop stamping live CDs and bootleg manufacturers were reported to be relocating, possibly to Australia or the Far East, or going underground in the UK and USA.

Although the first rock bootleg, *Great White Wonder*, was not released until 1969, concert-goers had been taping live shows before then by smuggling in portable tape recorders to make audience recordings. In later years, some live concerts were recorded at the soundboard, meaning a recording made from the mixing desk or PA system, although these recordings were relatively uncommon in the 60s due to non-existent or primitive PA systems. The growth in popularity of cassette tapes in the early 70s gave rise to tape collectors, and Bob Dylan's 1974 'comeback' tour is generally thought to be the first American tour to be recorded in its entirety from the audience.

There are several important differences between tape collectors and bootleggers. Tape collectors will generally trade tapes with other collectors rather than selling them. Collectors tend to circulate tapes in their original form, whereas bootleggers sometimes mix recordings from different locations, and occasionally release some rare tracks with previously available tracks for obvious commercial reasons. Tape collectors are usually dedicated fans, and they therefore place considerable importance on accurate information about the recordings, whereas the information on bootlegs is all too often incomplete or inaccurate. Sometimes the music on the bootleg is of poor recording quality or plays at the wrong speed, depending on the source of the bootleg. This can also be a problem for tape collectors, but generally collectors take more care over copying than bootleggers, and will circulate tapes in the best available quality.

Since at least the early 70s, bootlegs were significantly more expensive than official releases due to the relatively small numbers of each bootleg being made and the attendant legal risks. The 'protection gap' bootlegs have helped to push prices down – sometimes to less than an official CD – but the best advice before buying a bootleg is still to listen before you buy.

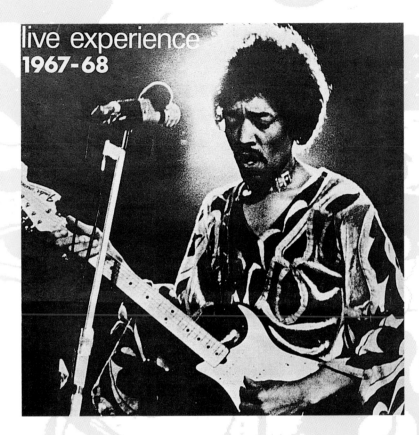

◀ The second major Hendrix bootleg LP, *Live Experience 1967–68*, was manufactured and sold in England. It was openly advertised in the press in late 1970, eventually resulting in a court case.

## ROOM FULL OF BOOTLEGS

The two main sources of Jimi Hendrix bootlegs, as with other artists, are live concerts and studio recordings, although the first Hendrix bootleg to appear on the market was actually from a jam session. 'Some cat went to a private practice [sic] session with a tiny tape recorder and made a pirate LP. The quality must be terrible,' said Jimi. 4,000 copies of *This Flyer* (USA, April 1970) were pressed, 3,000 for distribution in the USA, and the rest went to the UK. In addition to live concerts and studio recordings, Jimi made many television appearances and radio broadcasts, some of which were taped and subsequently released as bootlegs. The *Live Experience 1967-68* LP (UK, 1970) contained the Jimi Hendrix Experience's performance from the 'Happening With Lulu' TV show on 4 January 1969, and also some material recorded from the BBC's Radio 1.

In Jimi's case, live recordings are particularly interesting, because he wouldn't play a song the same way twice – ever. This constant improvisation in Jimi's work has even been the basic premise behind the official releases *Variations On A Theme: Red House* (USA, 1989) and the four-CD box set *Stages* (UK/USA, 1991). *Variations* brought together six different versions of 'Red House', and *Stages* consisted of four live performances from four consecutive years, which show Jimi's constant musical development.

From Jimi's arrival in London on 24 September 1966 to his death on 18 September 1970, he made 525 official concert appearances, of which nearly 130 have surfaced on tape, providing a large pool of live material for the bootlegger. Generally speaking, a tape is circulated among tape collectors until it ends up in the hands of an enterprising bootlegger who decides to manufacture a bootleg.

Although there are many official Jimi Hendrix live releases, very often the only way of hearing the complete performance of a concert in the correct order is on bootleg or an audience tape circulated by tape collectors. Of the four live shows released on the *Stages* four-CD box set, all four concerts had been previously available on bootleg or audience tape, but only two of the CDs contained complete concerts in the correct order. Similarly, the official *Woodstock* CD contains only ten tracks, compared to the fifteen tracks available on the *Woodstock Nation* bootleg double CD (Italy, 1989).

In addition to being incomplete, the official *Woodstock* CD changes the order of the songs – 'arranged and paced for flow' according to the sleeve notes – and alters the instrument mix. Larry Lee's rhythm guitar is kept low in the mix, as is the percussion playing of Juma Sultan and Jerry Velez; Larry's guitar solo in 'Red House' is simply edited out. Regardless of the aesthetic benefits of these alterations, the dedicated listener is being prevented from hearing a live performance 'as it was'.

Recording technology in the 60s was very basic when compared to the facilities available in the late 80s and early 90s, and some concerts were thus spoiled for official release as a result of technical shortcomings when the concert was recorded. Also, many of Jimi's live performances were plagued by equipment problems, such as amplifiers picking up stray radio signals or not working properly. Jimi's vigorous use of the vibrato arm often put his guitar out of tune, which might also prevent an otherwise good performance from being officially released.

The *Stages* and *Woodstock* CDs are examples of a crossover from a live recording previously available as bootleg or tape collector's tape to an official release, partly prompted by the continuing demand for new releases from an artist who is no longer producing new work. There is one notable exception of this process working the other way round, whereby an officially released album was released as a bootleg but in a different format – the official *Rainbow Bridge* LP was originally released in 1971, but has never been officially released on CD, prompting the release of the *Rainbow Bridge* bootleg CD (Holland, 1992).

Besides live recordings, the other major source of Jimi Hendrix bootlegs is studio recordings containing previously unheard new songs, alternate takes of known songs, and studio jams. The *Studio Haze* CD (USA, 1993) contained nine 'new' songs which were unearthed at Olympic Sound Studios in Barnes, London, where the Experience recorded in their early days. Chas Chandler considered some of the material suitable for release – 'So far I've discovered enough unheard songs to make at least one album...' – and Noel Redding and Mitch Mitchell recorded new bass and drum tracks on several songs in 1988. However, the official release of the tracks never materialized, due to disputes between the parties trying to arrange the release. The bootleg CD reveals the new songs as unfinished, and suggests that they could not have been released officially without major reworking and further overdubbing.

Studio bootlegs containing alternate takes of previously released songs offer interesting insights into an artist's creative process. The *Out Of The Studio: Demos From 1967* CD (UK, 1993) contains four versions of 'Red House', the last version being the take that was released in slightly different form on the US version of *Smash Hits*. *Out Of The Studio: Demos From 1967* also contains five different versions of 'I Don't Live Today', leading up to the basic version that was released on *Are You Experienced?*.

Jimi liked to record his studio jamming sessions with other musicians, and some of these recordings have been used for official releases such as *Nine To The Universe* (UK/USA, 1978). Jimi's jam with jazz guitarist John McLaughlin has been partly released on bootlegs such as *Record Plant Jam* (Italy, 1992), but many of these jams are interesting mainly as historical documents – the commercial release of a jam session would be the last thing on the musicians' minds when they were jamming. Jimi also recorded rough demos at home, as can be found on the *Acoustic Jams* double CD (Italy, 1989), recorded in his New York flat in early 1968 and in his Shokan house in Autumn 1969.

Jimi's studio work has not been comprehensively catalogued in the way that the Beatles' studio work was catalogued for Mark Lewisohn's book *The Complete Beatles Recording Sessions* (Hamlyn, 1988). The Beatles mainly used the same location, Abbey Road Studios, for recording, and EMI opened up the Abbey Road Studios archive for the project. Jimi used several different studios, thus making the logistics of such a project much more difficult, although not entirely impossible.

Considering Jimi's perfectionist nature and his cavalier attitude to money matters, he may have objected to commercial bootlegs more on artistic grounds than financial grounds. But his easy-going nature and regard for fans means that he probably wouldn't have objected to the network of tape collectors. For those familiar with Jimi's official releases, the world of tape collecting offers a considerable source of fascinating material, and also offers a whole new perspective on Jimi's art.

▲ Despite the added Japanese 'look', this bootleg CD of *Rainbow Bridge* was manufactured in Holland.

◄ This bootleg may cause damage to your CD player! The two CDs were simply *glued* together, thus making it much too heavy for a lot of CD players to handle.

These two pages represent various bootleg album covers from around the world – most are recordings from live performances.

1   LP, *Guitar Hero*, BBC material.

2   LP, *Pipe Dream*, The Amazing Kornyfone Records label, USA, late 1970s.

3   LP, Copenhagen, 1968.

5   LP, *Guitar Hero*, BBC material.

6   LP, *Wow*, Monterey 1967 and Woodstock 1969.

7   LP, *Sky High!*, 1968.

4   Double LP, *The Experience*, [aka Magic Fingers] Towne Records, USA, 1980.

11   LP, *Live in Ottaway* [sic] no label, USA, 1981.

8   LP, *Primal Keys*, BBC material.

9   LP, *Loaded Guitar*, Mixed.

10   LP, *Sky High*, 1968.

12   LP, *Live in Stockholm*, Fruit End, Holland, mid 1970s.

13   LP, *Jam*, Ax Records, USA, 1970s.

① LP, *Midnight Lightning*, Ottawa, 1968. Note Jimi's given name on the cover.

② LP, *Jimi Hendrix Live in Los Angeles Forum, CA., USA*, 1969.

③ LP, *Atlanta*, 1970.

④ LP, Last Bristish and American Concerts: Isle of Wright [sic] and Hawaii, 1970.

⑤ LP, Davenport, Iowa, 1968.

⑥ LP, *Midnight Magic*, San Diego, 1969.

⑦ LP, Randall's Island, 1970.

⑧ LP, *Hollywood Bowl*, 1968.

⑨ LP, *A Lifetime of Experience* (Gig/Newport) 1969.

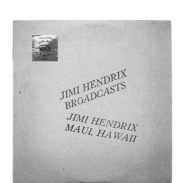

⑫ Double LP, *Jimi Hendrix Broadcasts/Jimi Hendrix Maui, Hawaii*.

⑩ LP, *Jimi Hendrix Live at the Hollywood Bowl, October 1968*.

⑪ LP, *Mannish Boy*, 1969.

▶ Double LP, *Jimi Hendrix Broadcasts/Jimi Hendrix Maui, Hawaii*. Note the 'Two Albums Cheap' distinction on the label – these may be cheap, but someone is certainly making a profit!

▲ A fantastic shot taken at the 'Star Club' in Hamburg, Germany – roadie Gerry Stickells is pushing Jimi's Marshall amp back, while manager Chas Chandler looks on at the right and drummer Mitch Mitchell plays to a crowd of enthusiastic fans. *March 1967*

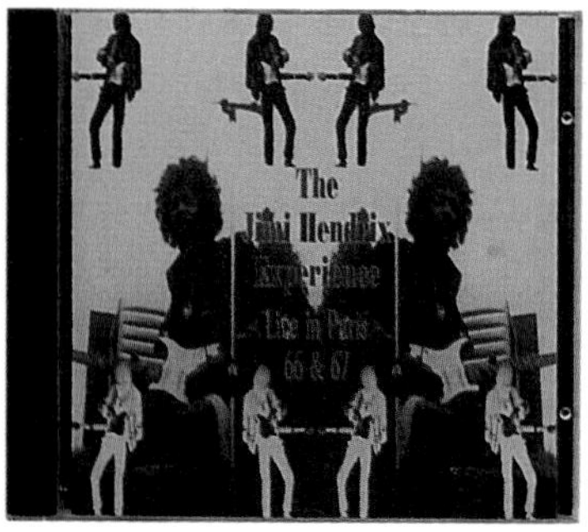


1

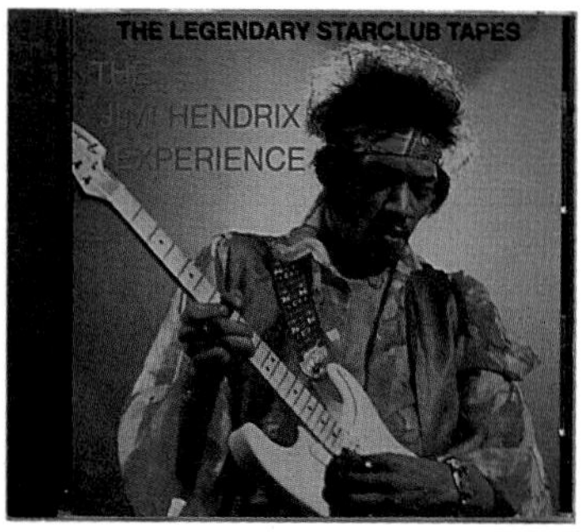


2

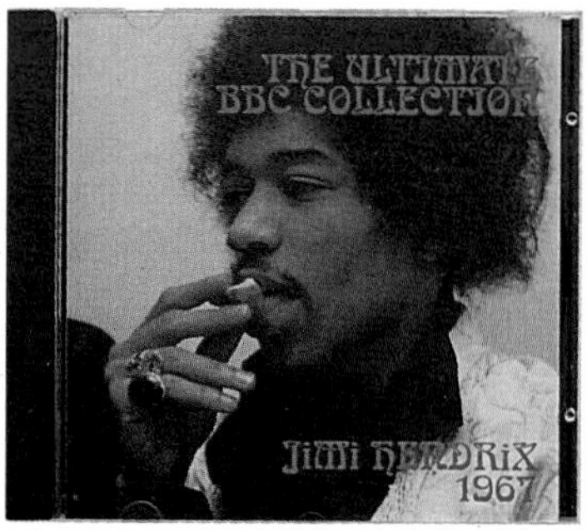


3

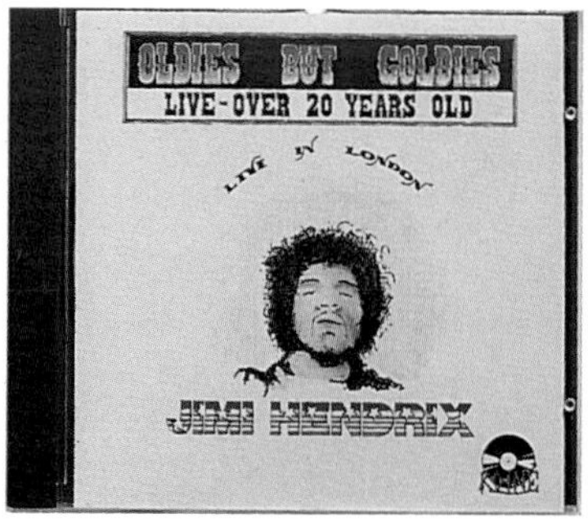


3

▲ Too hot to handle – from this page to page 193 are several Hendrix bootleg CDs that have been available on the market at various times.

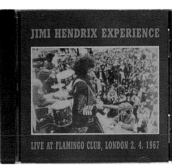

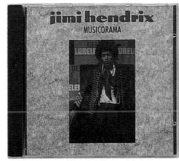

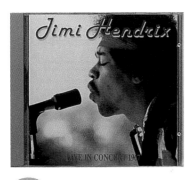

1. CD, *Live in Paris, 66 & 67*.

2. CD, *The Legendary Starclub Tapes* [sic], live, German radio, 18 March 1967.

3. Various bootleg CDs made from BBC concert material, 1967.

4. CD, *Have Mersy* [sic] *on Me Baby*, Flamingo Club recording, 4 February 1967.

5. CD, *Live at Flamingo Club* – same recordings as 4 above.

6. Various bootleg CDs made from Paris concert material, 1968.

7. CD, *Guitar Hero*, BBC, 1967.

8. CD, *Live in Stockholm*, 1967 and 1969 material.

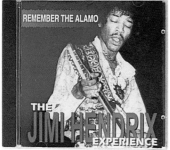

**1** Four bootleg CDs from Texas, 1968.

**2** Bootleg CDs of various New York gigs, including Café Au Go Go (top right), March 1968.

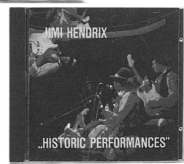

**3** Four bootleg CDs from Ottawa, Canada, 1968.

**4** Three bootleg CDs featuring jam sessions with B.B. King, 1968.

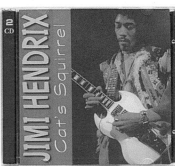

1   Two bootleg CDs of mixed sessions, 1968.

2   Two bootleg CDs with material from Sweden, 1969; and one from San Diego, 1969.

3   Two bootleg CDs from Stockholm, 1969.

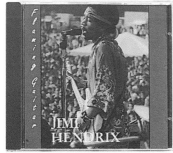

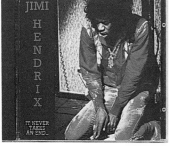
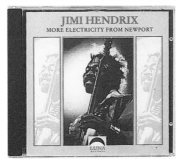

4   Various bootleg CDs from Los Angeles, 1969.

5   Four bootleg CDs from Newport, 1969.

6   CD, *Burning at Frankfurt*, 1969.

**1** CD, Denver, 1969.

**2** CD, Baltimore, 1970.

**3** *Shokan Sunrise* CD, Woodstock rehearsals, 1969.

**4** CD, live, mixed.

**5** Two CDs, Isle of Wight/Hawaii, 1970.

**6** CD, Baltimore Civic Centre, 13 June 1970.

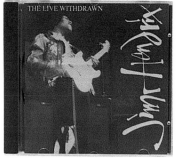

**7** Four CDs, Atlanta, 1970.

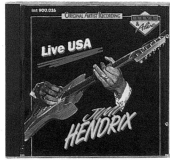

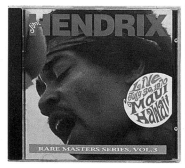

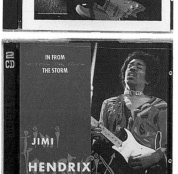

**8** Four CDs, Hawaii, 1970.

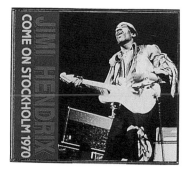

**1** Two bootleg CDs, Stockholm, 1970.

**2** Various bootleg CDs of mixed recordings/dates.

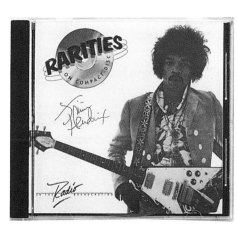
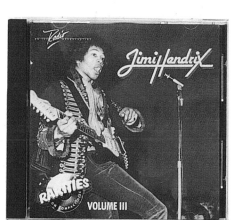

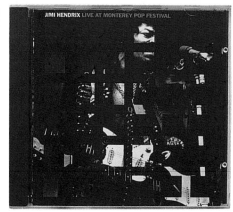

**3** Various bootleg CDs of mixed recordings/dates/places.

**1** LP, *Gypsy on Cloud Nine.*

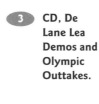

**2** LP, *Blues.*

**3** CD, De Lane Lea Demos and Olympic Outtakes.

**4** Two CDs, *The Wild Man of Pop Plays*, Volume 1 & Volume 2, Mixed live.

**5** CD, *Out of the Studio: Demo's From 1967* [sic].

**6** CD, *Demos From 1968.*

**7** LP, *Studio Haze.*

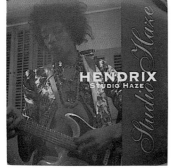

**9** Various bootleg CDs of mixed studio recordings.

**8** Three CDs from the Sotheby's Auction collection of tapes and private reels.

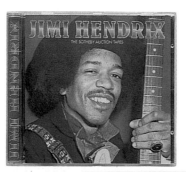

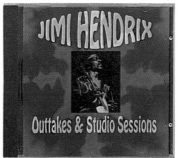

**1** CD, *Electric Ladyland Outtakes.* Studio bootleg recording.

**2** CD, *Talent & Feeling Vol.1.*

**3** Two CDs, bootlegs of Band of Gypsys recordings.

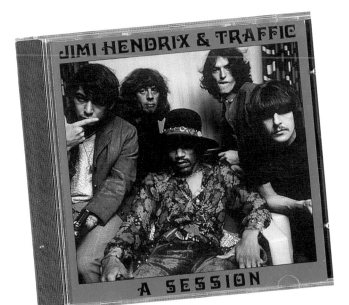

**4** CD, *A Session.* Bootleg studio recording with Traffic.

**5** Bootleg CDs, *Talent & Feeling Vol. 2, Paper Airplanes, Jimi Hendrix Live!, Gypsy Suns, Moons and Rainbows.* All are mixed, mainly studio, with the exception of the one live recording.

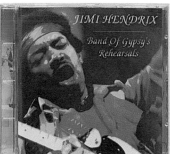

▶ Four CDs, all bootleg recordings of Band of Gypsys.

▲▶ **(This page and opposite) Various bootleg CDs of mixed studio recordings.**

▲ The *"Drone Blues"* bootleg CD was released together with the magazine *Satisfaction* (Italy, 1993).

◀ Four bootleg CDs containing studio outtakes recorded between 1968 and 1970.

▲ ▶ Three bootleg picture discs.

1

Box set from Luxembourg, 1994.

Box set from Italy, 1993.

The four CDs included with the above Italian bootleg box.

3

1  Front and back of a box set from Italy (1995) – it comes with two CDs and ten photographs lifted from a photobook.

2  The two CDs included with the above box.

3  Yet another Italian job from late 1993 – this one contains eight CDs, plus a poor video and book.

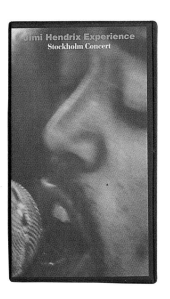

1 **And now for something completely different: two CDs stuck onto cardboard!**

2 **These two bootleg CDs come in a rather heavy metal case.**

3 **Four of the CDs plus the video from the *51st Anniversary* box reproduced on the opposite page.**

# 9

# TOUR DATES

"Every day in the

week I'm in a

different city...."

*Jimi Hendrix*, Stone Free

**NOTE:** ' – 2 ' indicates the band performed two separate shows in the same venue, but to a new audience. However, in late 1966 and early 1967, the band would play two sets to the same audience with a break between sets.

## 1966

### OCTOBER
13 **Evreux**, France, Novelty
14 **Nancy**, France, unconfirmed venue
15 **Villerupt**, France, Salle Des Fêtes
18 **Paris**, France, Olympia
  From 13 to 18: touring as support act with Johnny Hallyday.
25 **London**, England, Scotch Of St James

### NOVEMBER
8 **München**, Germany, Big Apple –2
9 **München**, Germany, Big Apple –2
10 **München**, Germany, Big Apple –2
11 **München**, Germany, Big Apple –2
25 **London**, Kingly Street, England, Bag O' Nails [press concert]
26 **Hounslow**, Middlesex, England, Ricky Tick

### DECEMBER
10 **London**, Brixton Road, Brixton, England, The Ram Jam Club
16 **Bromley**, Kent, England, Chislehurst Caves
21 **London**, Queen's Gate, Kensington, England, Blaises
22 **Southampton**, Hampshire, England, GuildHall –2
26 **London**, Forest Gate, England, The Upper Cut
31 **Folkestone**, Kent, England, Hillside Social Club

## 1967

### JANUARY
4 **Bromley**, Kent, England, Bromel Club/Bromley Court Hotel –2
7 **Manchester**, Lancashire, England, New Century Hall
8 **Sheffield**, Yorkshire, England, Mojo A Go-Go/Tollbar
11 **London**, Kingly Street, England, Bag O'Nails –2
12 **London**, Whitehorse Street, England, 7 ½ Club
13 **London**, Whitehorse Street, England, 7 ½ Club
14 **Nottingham**, Nottinghamshire, England, Beachcomber Club
15 **Kirk Levington**, Yorkshire, England, Country Club

16 **London**, Whitehorse Street, England, 7 ½ Club
17 **London**, Oxford Street, England, Tiles/'Ready,Steady, Radio!'
17 **London**, Whitehorse Street, England, 7 ½ Club
18 **London**, Whitehorse Street, England, 7 ½ Club
19 **London**, Margaret Street, England, Speakeasy
20 **London**, Hampstead, England, Haverstock Country Hill Club
21 **London**, Golders Green, England, Refectory
22 **Oldham**, Lancashire, England, The Astoria
24 **London**, Wardour Street, England, Marquee
25 **Norwich**, Norfolk, England, Orford Cellar
27 **Bromley**, Kent, England, Chislehurst Caves
28 **London**, Forest Gate, England, The Upper Cut
29 **London**, Shaftesbury Avenue, England, Saville Theatre –2

### FEBRUARY
1 **South Shields**, Durham, England, New Cellar Club
2 **Darlington**, Durham, England, Imperial Club/Imperial Hotel
3 **Hounslow**, Middlesex, England, Ricky Tick
4 **London**, Brixton Road, Brixton, England, The Ram Jam Club
4 **London**, Wardour Street, England, The Flamingo Club
6 **Croydon**, Surrey, England, Star Hotel
8 **Bromley**, Kent, England, Bromley Club/Bromley Court Hotel
9 **Bristol**, Gloucestershire, England, Locarno
10 **Newbury**, Berkshire, England, Plaza
11 **Cheltenham**, Gloucestershire, England, Blue Moon
12 **Stockport**, Cheshire, England, Sinking Ship Clubland
14 **Grays**, Essex, England, The Civic Hall
15 **Cambridge**, Cambridgeshire, England, Dorothy Ballroom
17 **Windsor**, Berkshire, England, Ricky Tick/Thames Hotel
18 **York**, Yorkshire, England, University
19 **London**, Tottenham Court Road, England, Blarney Club
20 **Bath**, Somerset, England, The Pavilion
22 **London**, Chalk Farm, England, Roundhouse
23 **Worthing**, Sussex, England, The Pavilion
24 **Leicester**, Leicestershire, England, University
25 **Chelmsford**, Essex, England, Corn Exchange
26 **Southend-on-Sea**, Essex, England, Cliffs Pavilion –2

▼ *Melody Maker* (England), 4 February 1967, review of joint concert with The Who as advertised above.

**Caught In The Act**

**Jimi Hendrix–Who battle at Saville**
mm 4-2-67

JIMI HENDRIX v the Who! It was a close battle at London's Saville Theatre on Sunday, and fans will still be arguing about the winners. Either way, two of Britain's most exciting groups thrilled the crowds with hard-hitting sights and sounds. After the Koobas and Thoughts came the Experience. And what an experience! Jimi was hit by PA trouble, but the crowd were so keyed up they laughed sympathetically while Jimi searched for a mike that worked. He stormed through "Like A Rolling Stone", "Can You See Me", "Hey Joe", and the incredible "Wild Thing", ending in a freak-out of guitar biting, feedback and uproar. "Follow that", was the feeling. Then came the Who — wild and unpredictable as ever. They played their best for months. Gone were smoke bombs and amplifier smashing. In their place were good singing and playing. There was still violence — John Entwistle took delight in kicking to pieces a miniature walking doll with flashing lights. During these incidents, Keith in flowered shirt and red trousers sang "Barbara Ann" John groaned "Boris The Spider", and Roger and Pete gave the seal to a great show with the Who mini-opera "A Quick One While He's Away" — CHRIS WELCH.

▶ **Tune-up-time –
backstage at the
Saville Theatre,
London.**
*29 January 1967*

**PLAZA
NEWBURY**

**JIMI
HENDRIX
EXPERIENCE**

**FRI. 10 FEB. 7'6**

**THE CIVIC HALL, GRAYS**

**TUESDAY, FEBRUARY 7**
THE GREAT COLOURED RAM JAM SOUND OF

**THE GASS**

**TUESDAY, FEBRUARY 14**
YOU DARE NOT MISS THE DISCOVERIES OF '67
THE

**JIMI HENDRIX**
EXPERIENCE

Smashing up the charts with "Hey Joe"
FROM 8 P.M. COME EARLY TO BE SURE OF GETTING IN

**THE PAVILION
WORTHING**

Thursday, Feb. 23rd
UNBELIEVABLE

**THE JIMMI HENDRIX
EXPERIENCE**
(HEY JOE)

ADMISSION 6/-
7.30 to 10.45 p.m.

**ROUNDHOUSE**
Chalk Farm Road, N.W.1
Wednesday, February 22nd, 7.30-11.30
the
**JIMI HENDRIX**
EXPERIENCE
and
**THE FLIES**
with
SANDY & HILARY
Tickets: 5/- in advance or 6/6 at the door

◀ **(Opposite page) Hendrix and Co.
loved performing in Paris, France, at
the famous Olympia venue. In 1966,
they performed as a completely
unknown support act, but one year
later they had already become
headliners.**
*'Olympia', Paris, 9 October 1967*

BOB ANTHONY PROMOTION
**CORN EXCHANGE** • CHELMSFORD          8 to 11.30 p.m.

**Saturday
Scene**

FEBRUARY 25th
"HEY JOE"
**The JIMI HENDRIX
EXPERIENCE**
Plus! THE SOUL TRINITY

Admission: 8/6 in advance. Tickets Corn Exchange
10/- on the night

**1967**

## MARCH

**1 Purley**, Surrey, England, Orchid Ballroom

**4 Colombes**, near Paris, France, Omnibus

**4 Paris**, France, Faculté de Droit d'Assas/Law Society Graduation Ball

**5 Mouscron**, Belgium, Twenty Club

**5 Lens**, France, Twenty Club

**9 Hull**, Yorkshire, England, Skyline Ballroom

**10 Newcastle-upon-Tyne**, Northumberland, England, Club À Go Go –2

**11 Leeds**, Yorkshire, England, International Club

**12 Ilkley**, Yorkshire, England, Gyro Club/Troutbeck Hotel

**17 Hamburg**, Germany, Star Club

**18 Hamburg**, Germany, Star Club –2

**19 Hamburg**, Germany, Star Club –2

**23 Southampton**, Hampshire, England, Guild Hall

**25 Boston**, Lincolnshire, England, Starlight Room/Gliderdrome

**26 Stockport**, Cheshire, England, Tabernacle Club

**28 Aylesbury**, Buckinghamshire, England, Assembly Hall

**31 London**, Finsbury Park, England, The Astoria –2

## APRIL

**1 Ipswich**, Suffolk, England, Gaumont –2

**2 Worcester**, Worcestershire, England, Gaumont –2

**5 Leeds**, Yorkshire, England, Odeon –2

**6 Glasgow**, Lanark, Scotland, Odeon –2

**7 Carlisle**, Cumberland, England, A.B.C. –2

**8 Chesterfield**, Derby, England, A.B.C. –2

**9 Liverpool**, Lancashire, England, The Empire –2

**11 Bedford**, Bedfordshire, England, Granada –2

**12 Southampton**, Hampshire, England, Gaumont –2

**13 Wolverhampton**, Staffordshire, England, Gaumont –2

**14 Bolton**, Lancashire, England, Odeon –2

**15 Blackpool**, Lancashire, England, Odeon –2

**16 Leicester**, Leicestershire, England, De Montfort Hall –2

**19 Birmingham**, Warwickshire, England, Odeon –2

**20 Lincoln**, Lincolnshire, England, A.B.C. –2

**21 Newcastle-upon-Tyne**, Northumberland, England, City Hall –2

**22 Manchester**, Lancashire, England, Odeon –2

**23 Hanley**, Staffordshire, England, Gaumont –2

**25 Bristol**, Gloucestershire, England, Colston Hall –2

**26 Cardiff**, Glamorgan, Wales, Capitol –2

**27 Aldershot**, Hampshire, England, A.B.C. –2

**28 Slough**, Buckinghamshire, England, Adelphi –2

**29 Bournemouth**, Dorset, England, Winter Gardens –2

**30 London**, Tooting, England, Granada –2

**From 31 March to 30 April**: package tour with Walker Brothers, Jimi Hendrix Experience, Cat Stevens, Engelbert Humperdinck, Californians, and Quottations.

## MAY

**6 Nelson**, Lancashire, England, Imperial Ballroom

**7 London**, Shaftesbury Avenue, England, Saville Theatre –2

**12 London**, England, Bluesville Club/Manor House

**13 London**, Kensington, England, Imperial College

**14 Manchester**, Lancashire, England, Belle Vue/New Elizabethan

**15 Berlin**, Germany, Neue Welt –2

**16 München**, Germany, Big Apple –2

**19 Göteborg**, Sweden, Konserthallen/Liseberg/ Lisebergs Nöjespark –2

**20 Karlstad**, Sweden, Mariebergsskogen

**21 Copenhagen**, Denmark, Falkoner Centret

**22 Helsinki**, Finland, Kulttuuritalo

**23 Malmö**, Sweden, Klubb Bongo – New Orleans–2

**24 Stockholm**, Sweden, Stora Scenen/Gröna Lund/Tivoli Garden

**24 Stockholm**, Sweden, Jump In/Gröna Lund/ Tivoli Garden

**27 Kiel**, Germany, Star Palace –2

**28 Herford**, Germany, Jaguar Club/Scala

**29 Spalding**, Lincolnshire, England, Tulip Bulb Auction Hall/ Barbeque '67

## JUNE

**4 London**, Shaftesbury Avenue, England, Saville Theatre –2

**18 Monterey**, California, USA, Monterey International Pop Festival

**20 San Francisco**, California, USA, Fillmore West –2

**21 San Francisco**, California, USA, Fillmore West –2

**22 San Francisco**, California, USA, Fillmore West –2

**23 San Francisco**, California, USA, Fillmore West –2

**24 San Francisco**, California, USA, Fillmore West –2

**25 San Francisco**, California, USA, The Panhandle/Golden Gate Park [free concert]

**25 San Francisco**, California, USA, Fillmore West –2

▲ **Entertainment provided for law school graduates in Paris.**
*4 March 1967*

▼ **Jimi visited Holland in March and November 1967, resulting twenty years later in a special feature in *Oor* magazine, 4 April 1987.**

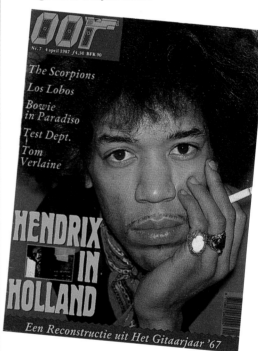

◀ Jimi in full concert-flight at the Star Club, Hamburg, Germany.
*March 1967*

▼ Jimi and Mitch (using a second bass drum borrowed from the support act) in action at the Neue Welt in Berlin.
*15 May 1967*

▲ Packing time just minutes after the above concert at the Star Club was completed.

**BARBEQUE '67**
TULIP BULB AUCTION HALL, SPALDING, LINCS.
SPRING BANK HOLIDAY MONDAY MAY 29th, 4.00 p.m.-12 p.m.
**JIMI HENDRIX EXPERIENCE**
**GENO WASHINGTON AND THE RAM JAM BAND**
**THE CREAM**
ZOOT MONEY AND HIS BIG ROLL BAND
PINK FLOYD • MOVE
Admission **£1** pay at door or tickets by post. Send s.a.e. to:
RIVONIA, 2 Conery Gardens, Whatton, Notts.

**1967**

### JULY

**1 Santa Barbara**, California, USA, Earl Warren
    Showgrounds
**2 Los Angeles**, California, USA, Whiskey A Go Go
**3 New York City**, New York, USA, Scene Club
**4 New York City**, New York, USA, Scene Club
**5 New York City**, New York, USA, Central Park/
    Rheingold Festival
**8 Jacksonville**, Florida, USA, Jacksonville Coliseum
**9 Miami**, Florida, USA, Miami Convention Hall
**11 Charlotte**, North Carolina, USA, Charlotte
    Coliseum
**12 Greensboro**, North Carolina, USA, Coliseum
**14 New York City**, Forest Hills, New York, USA,
    Forest Hills Stadium
**15 New York City**, Forest Hills, New York, USA,
    Forest Hills Stadium
**16 New York City**, Forest Hills, New York, USA,
    Forest Hills Stadium
**From 8 to 16:** touring as support act with the
    Monkees
**20 New York City**, Greenwich Village, New York,
    USA, Salvation
**21 New York City**, Greenwich Village, New York,
    USA, Café Au Go Go −2
**22 New York City**, Greenwich Village, New York,
    USA, Café Au Go Go −2
**23 New York City**, Greenwich Village, New York,
    USA, Café Au Go Go −2

### AUGUST

**3 New York City**, Greenwich Village, New York,
    USA, Salvation
**4 New York City**, Greenwich Village, New York,
    USA, Salvation
**5 New York City**, Greenwich Village, New York,
    USA, Salvation
**7 New York City**, Greenwich Village, New York,
    USA, Salvation
**8 New York City**, Greenwich Village, New York,
    USA, Salvation
**9 Washington DC**, USA, Ambassador Theatre −2
**10 Washington DC**, USA, Ambassador Theatre −2
**11 Washington DC**, USA, Ambassador Theatre −2
**12 Washington DC**, USA, Ambassador Theatre −2
**13 Washington DC**, USA, Ambassador Theatre/
    Keep The Faith For Washington Youth
    Fund −2
**15 Ann Arbor**, Michigan, USA, Fifth Dimension
    Club −2
**18 Hollywood**, California, USA, Hollywood Bowl
**19 Santa Barbara**, California, USA, Earl Warren
    Showgrounds

**27 London**, Shaftesbury Avenue, England, Saville
    Theatre
**29 Nottingham**, Nottinghamshire, England,
    Sherwood Rooms/Nottingham Blues
    Festival

### SEPTEMBER

**3 Göteborg**, Sweden, Konserthallen/Liseberg/
    Lisebergs Nöjespark −2
**4 Stockholm**, Sweden, Stora Scenen/Gröna Lund/
    Tivoli Garden
**4 Stockholm**, Sweden, Dans In/Gröna Lund/Tivoli
    Garden
**6 Västerås**, Sweden, Västerås Idrottshall −2
**8 Högbo**, Sweden, Högbo Bruk/Popladan −2
**9 Karlstad**, Sweden, Mariebergsskogen −2
**10 Lund**, Sweden, Stora Salen/Akademiska
    Föreningen −2
**11 Stockholm**, Sweden, Stora Scenen/Gröna Lund/
    Tivoli Garden
**11 Stockholm**, Sweden, Dans In/Gröna Lund/
    Tivoli Garden
**12 Göteborg**, Sweden, Stjärnscenen/Liseberg/
    Lisebergs Nöjespark −2
**25 London**, England, Royal Festival Hall/'Guitar-In'

▲ **Jimi was extremely popular in
Sweden. Here he's pictured with a
rarely seen Fender guitar with a
tortoiseshell pickguard (not to mention
his Micky Mouse button!) −
Konserthallen/Liseberg, Göteborg.**
*3 September 1967*

◀ All three concert dates of the Jimi Hendrix Experience at the Olympia in Paris were recorded by Radio station Europe 1, with highlights being broadcast during the programme *Musicorama*.

*9 October 1967*

**OCTOBER**

**7 Dereham**, Norfolk, England, The Wellington Club

**8 London**, Shaftesbury Avenue, England, Saville Theatre −2

**9 Paris**, France, Olympia

**15 Crawley**, Sussex, England, Starlight Ballroom

**22 Hastings**, Sussex, England, Hastings Pier

**24 London**, Wardour Street, England, Marquee

**28 Dunstable**, Bedfordshire, England, California Ballroom

**HASTINGS PIER**
SUNDAY CLUB
General Manager: R. E. Knights          Tel. Hastings 2566
**SUNDAY, 22nd OCTOBER**
**7.30 - 11**
**JIMI HENDRIX EXPERIENCE**
PLUS
**FULL SUPPORTING PROGRAM**
**TICKETS IN ADVANCE 12/6**
**(AT DOOR ON NIGHT 15/-)**
REFRESHMENT BARS AND FULLY LICENSED BUFFET
ADVANCE TICKETS ARE ON SALE FROM
**1st** OCTOBER AT PIER BOX OFFICE
BOOK EARLY!     GET YOUR TICKET TODAY!

▲▼ Two magazine covers with Paris 1967 photographs – *Guitar Heroes*, France, 1992; and *The History of Rock*, England, 1983.

▼ The *Guitar World* (France) magazine from 1990 came with a CD (below, centre, *Hendrix Inedit*) with twelve very short samples from the various Hal Leonard (USA) CD releases.

## 1967

### NOVEMBER

**8 Manchester**, Lancashire, England, The Union

**10 Rotterdam**, Holland, Ahoy Hallen/Hippy Happy Beurs Voor Tieners en Twens

**11 Brighton**, Sussex, England, Sussex University/New Refectory

**14 London**, England, Royal Albert Hall

**15 Bournemouth**, Hampshire, England, Winter Gardens –2

**17 Sheffield**, Yorkshire, England, City Hall –2

**18 Liverpool**, Lancashire, England, Empire Theatre –2

**19 Coventry**, Warwickshire, England, The Coventry Theatre –2

**22 Portsmouth**, Hampshire, England, Guild Hall –2

**23 Cardiff**, Glamorgan, Wales, Sophia Gardens Pavilion –2

**24 Bristol**, Gloucestershire, England, Colston Hall –2

**25 Blackpool**, Lancashire, England, Opera House –2

**26 Manchester**, Lancashire, England, Palace Theatre –2

**27 Belfast**, N. Ireland, Whitla Hall/Queens College/Festival Of Arts –2

### DECEMBER

**1 Chatham**, Kent, England, Central Hall –2

**2 Brighton**, Sussex, England, The Dome –2

**3 Nottingham**, Nottinghamshire, England, Theatre Royal – 2

**4 Newcastle-upon-Tyne**, Northumberland, England, City Hall –2

**5 Glasgow**, Lanark, Scotland, Green's Playhouse –2

**From 14 November to 5 December:** package tour with Jimi Hendrix Experience, The Move, Pink Floyd, Amen Corner, Outer Limits, Eire Apparent, and The Nice.

**22 London**, Kensington, England, Olympia/ 'Christmas On Earth Continued'

◀ Two concert hall photos taken just four days and one hat apart – Ahoy Hallen, Rotterdam, Holland, 10 November 1967 (far left) and Royal Albert Hall, London, 14 November 1967.

▶ Classic shot of Jimi with his white Fender Stratocaster. Unknown venue, New York.
*August 1968*

▶ Great op-art design poster for the Experience's Fillmore East concert, 10 May 1968.

▼ Front cover of magazine *Record Review* (USA), October 1980, graced with a nice photo of Jimi at the Miami Pop Festival, 18 May 1968. The second day of the festival was cancelled due to bad weather.

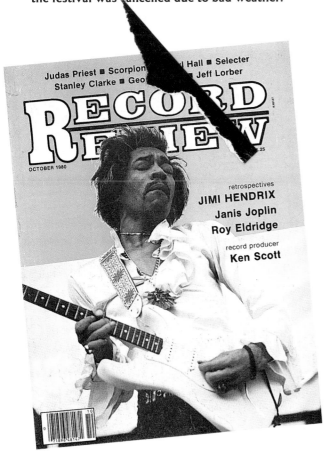

▼ Jimi's one and only visit to Switzerland resulted in tons of fine photographs – this one was taken during the Hallenstadion show of 30 May 1968.

# 1968

## JULY

**6 Woburn Abbey**, Bedfordshire, England, Woburn Music Festival

**15 Palma**, Majorca, Spain, Sgt. Peppers

**30 Baton Rouge**, Louisiana, USA, Independence Hall/Lakeshore Auditorium −2

**31 Shreveport**, Louisiana, USA, Municipal Auditorium

## AUGUST

**1 New Orleans**, Louisiana, USA, City Park Stadium

**2 San Antonio**, Texas, USA, Municipal Auditorium

**3 Dallas**, Texas, USA, Moody Coliseum/Southern Methodist University

**4 Houston**, Texas, USA, Sam Houston Coliseum

**10 Chicago**, Illinois, USA, Auditorium Theatre −2

**11 Davenport**, Iowa, USA, Col Ballroom

**16 Columbia**, Maryland, USA, Merriweather Post Pavilion

**17 Atlanta**, Georgia, USA, Atlanta Municipal Auditorium −2

**18 Tampa**, Florida, USA, Curtis Hixon Hall

**20 Richmond**, Virginia, USA, The Mosque −2

**21 Virginia Beach**, Virginia, USA, Civic Dome −2

**23 New York City**, Queens, New York, USA, Singer Bowl/Flushing Meadow Park/The New York Rock Festival

**24 Hartford**, Connecticut, USA, Bushnell Memorial

**25 Framingham**, Massachusetts, USA, Carousel Theatre −2

**26 Bridgeport**, Connecticut, USA, Kennedy Stadium

**30 Salt Lake City**, Utah, USA, Lagoon Opera House

## SEPTEMBER

**1 Denver**, Colorado, USA, Red Rocks Park

**3 San Diego**, California, USA, Balbao Stadium

**4 Phoenix**, Arizona, USA, Memorial Coliseum

**5 San Bernardino**, California, USA, Swing Auditorium

**6 Seattle**, Washington, USA, Center Coliseum

**7 Vancouver**, British Columbia, Canada, Pacific Coliseum

**8 Spokane**, Washington, USA, Coliseum

**9 Portland**, Oregon, USA, Memorial Coliseum

**13 Oakland**, California, USA, Oakland Coliseum

**14 Hollywood**, California, USA, Hollywood Bowl

**15 Sacramento**, California, USA, Memorial Auditorium

## OCTOBER

**5 Honolulu**, Island of Oahu, Hawaii, USA, Honolulu International Center

**10 San Francisco**, California, USA, Winterland −2

**11 San Francisco**, California, USA, Winterland −2

**12 San Francisco**, California, USA, Winterland −2

**26 Bakersfield**, California, USA, Civic Auditorium

## NOVEMBER

**1 Kansas City**, Missouri, USA, Municipal Auditorium Arena

**2 Minneapolis**, Minnesota, USA, Auditorium

**3 St Louis**, Missouri, USA, Kiel Auditorium

**15 Cincinnati**, Ohio, USA, Cincinnati Gardens

**16 Boston**, Massachusetts, USA, Boston Garden

**17 New Haven**, Connecticut, USA, Yale University/Woolsey Hall

**22 Jacksonville**, Florida, USA, Jacksonville Coliseum

**23 Tampa**, Florida, USA, Curtis Hixon Hall

**24 Miami Beach**, Florida, USA, Convention Hall

**27 Providence**, Rhode Island, USA, Rhode Island Auditorium

**28 New York City**, New York, USA, Philharmonic Hall −2

**30 Detroit**, Michigan, USA, Cobo Arena

## DECEMBER

**1 Chicago**, Illinois, USA, Coliseum

▲▼ Advertisement and action shot for a concert at the Singer Bowl, New York City.

*23 August 1968*

▲ Concert flyer for Jimi's second concert in Seattle during 1968.

▼ 'Schedule of Events' card listing a concert in Portland.

◀ Woolsey Hall/Yale University, New Haven, Connecticut.
*17 November 1968*

▼ Bootleg LP containing recordings from the Philharmonic Hall concert in New York City.

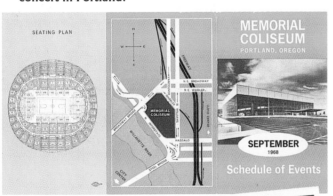

# 1969

### JANUARY

**8 Göteborg**, Sweden, Lorensberg Cirkus −2

**9 Stockholm**, Sweden, Konserthuset −2

**10 Copenhagen**, Denmark, Falkoner Centret −2

**11 Hamburg**, Germany, Musikhalle −2

**12 Düsseldorf**, Germany, Rheinhalle −2

**13 Köln**, Germany, Sporthalle

**14 Münster**, Germany, Halle Münsterland

**15 München**, Germany, Kongreßsaal/ Deutsches Museum −2

**16 Nürnberg**, Germany, Meistersingerhalle −2

**17 Frankfurt**, Germany, Jahrhunderthalle −2

**19 Stuttgart**, Germany, Liederhalle −2

**21 Strasbourg**, France, Wacken/Hall 16

**22 Wien**, Austria, Konzerthaus/Stimmen Der Welt −2

**23 Berlin**, Germany, Sportpalast

▲ **Lorensberg Cirkus, Göteborg, Sweden.**

*8 January 1969*

▼ **Jimi playing a white Gibson SG – Falkoner Centret, Copenhagen, Denmark.**

*10 January 1969*

**FEBRUARY**

**18 London**, England, Royal Albert Hall

**24 London**, England, Royal Albert Hall

**April**

**11 Raleigh**, North Carolina, USA, Dorton Arena

**12 Philadelphia**, Pennsylvania, USA, Spectrum

**18 Memphis**, Tennessee, USA, Ellis Auditorium Amphitheatre −2

**19 Houston**, Texas, USA, Sam Houston Coliseum

**20 Dallas**, Texas, USA, Memorial Auditorium

**26 Los Angeles**, California, USA, The Forum

**27 Oakland**, California, USA, Oakland Coliseum

**MAY**

**2 Detroit**, Michigan, USA, Convention Arena/Cobo Arena

**3 Toronto**, Ontario, Canada, Maple Leaf Gardens

**4 Syracuse**, New York, USA, Syracuse War Memorial Auditorium

**7 Tuscaloosa**, Alabama, USA, Memorial Auditorium

**9 Charlotte**, North Carolina, USA, Charlotte Coliseum

**10 Charleston**, West Virginia, USA, Charleston Civic Center

**11 Indianapolis**, Indiana, USA, Fairgrounds Coliseum

**16 Baltimore**, Maryland, USA, Civic Center

**17 Providence**, Rhode Island, USA, Rhode Island Auditorium

**18 New York City**, New York, USA, Madison Square Garden

**23 Seattle**, Washington, USA, Seattle Coliseum

**24 San Diego**, California, USA, Sports Arena

**25 San Jose**, California, USA, Santa Clara County Fairgrounds/Pop Festival

**30 Honolulu**, Island of Oahu, Hawaii, USA, Waikiki Shell

**31 Honolulu**, Island of Oahu, Hawaii, USA, Waikiki Shell

**JUNE**

**1 Honolulu**, Island of Oahu, Hawaii, USA, Waikiki Shell

**20 San Fernando** [nearby], Devonshire Downs, north of San Fernando Valley, California, USA/Newport 69

**29 Denver**, Colorado, USA, Mile High Stadium/Denver Pop Festival

**AUGUST**

**18 Bethel**, New York, USA, Woodstock Music And Art Fair

**SEPTEMBER**

**5 New York City**, 139th Street/Lanox Avenue, Harlem, New York, USA [jazz festival on the street/Benefit for the United Block Association]

**10 New York City**, New York, USA, Salvation

**DECEMBER**

**31 New York City**, New York, USA, Fillmore East −2

▲ **The Jimi Hendrix Experience played two sold-out shows at the Royal Albert Hall in London during February 1969. A film was made during the show on the 24th, where this photo was taken, but Hendrix fans are still waiting for its official release.**

◄ **Live at the Spectrum, Philadelphia, Pennsylvania, USA.**
*12 April 1969*

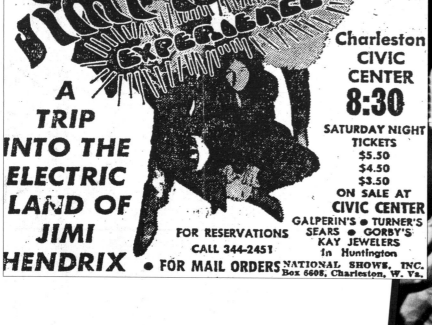

▼ **Jimi in action during a benefit concert for the United Block Association in Harlem.**
*5 September 1969*

► **Four shows by the Band of Gypsys at Bill Graham's Fillmore East venue in New York City resulted in the live LP *Band Of Gypsys* released in April 1970.**
*31 December 1969*

# 1970

### JANUARY
**1 New York City**, New York, USA, Fillmore East −2
**28 New York City**, New York, USA, Madison Square Garden/Winter Festival For Peace

### APRIL
**25 Los Angeles**, California, USA, The Forum
**26 Sacramento**, California, USA, Cal Expo

### MAY
**1 Milwaukee**, Wisconsin, USA, Milwaukee Auditorium
**2 Madison**, Wisconsin, USA, Dane County Memorial Coliseum
**3 St. Paul**, Minnesota, USA, St. Paul Civic Center
**4 New York City**, New York, USA, Village Gate/Holding Together [Benefit for Timothy Leary]
**8 Norman**, Oklahoma, USA, University Of Oklahoma Field House −2
**9 Fort Worth**, Texas, USA, Will Rogers Coliseum
**10 San Antonio**, Texas, USA, San Antonio Hemisphere Arena
**16 Philadelphia**, Pennsylvania, USA, Temple University Stadium
**30 Berkeley**, California, USA, Berkeley Community Theatre −2

### JUNE
**5 Dallas**, Texas, USA, Memorial Auditorium
**6 Houston**, Texas, USA, Sam Houston Coliseum
**7 Tulsa**, Oklahoma, USA, Assembly Center Arena
**9 Memphis**, Tennessee, USA, Mid-South Coliseum
**10 Evansville**, Indiana, USA, Roberts Municipal Stadium
**13 Baltimore**, Maryland, USA, Civic Center
**19 Albuquerque**, New Mexico, USA, Civic Auditorium −2

**20 San Bernardino**, California, USA, Swing Auditorium
**21 Ventura**, California, USA, Ventura County Fairgrounds
**23 Denver**, Colorado, USA, Mammoth Gardens
**27 Boston**, Massachusetts, USA, Boston Garden

### JULY
**4 Byron** [nearby], Georgia, USA, Middle Georgia Raceway/'2nd Atlanta International Pop Festival'
**5 Miami**, Florida, USA, Miami Jai Alai Fronton −2
**17 New York**, Randall's Island, New York, USA, Downing Stadium/New York Pop
**25 San Diego**, California, USA, Sports Arena
**26 Seattle**, Washington, USA, Sicks Stadium
**30 Haleakala Crater** [nearby Seabury Hall], Rainbow Ridge, Island of Maui, Hawaii, USA/'Rainbow Bridge Vibratory Color/Sound Experiment' −2

### AUGUST
**1 Honolulu**, Isle of Oahu, Hawaii, USA, Arena/Honolulu International Center
**30 Isle of Wight**, England, Isle of Wight Festival
**31 Stockholm**, Sweden, Stora Scenen/Gröna Lund/Tivoli Garden

### SEPTEMBER
**1 Göteborg**, Sweden, Stora Scenen/Liseberg
**2 Århus**, Denmark, Vejlby-Risskov Hallen
**3 Copenhagen**, Denmark, K.B. Hallen
**4 Berlin**, Germany, Deutschlandhalle/Super Concert '70
**6 Isle of Fehmarn**, Germany, Love And Peace Festival

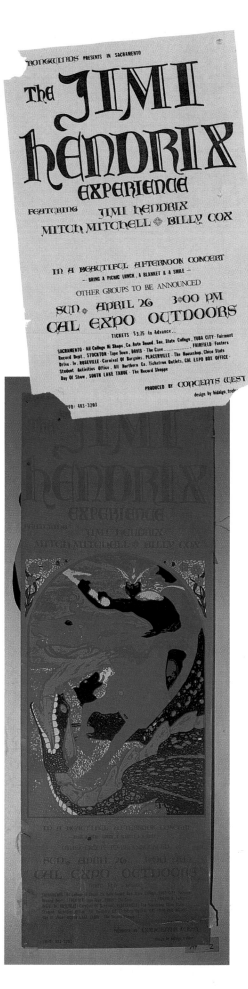

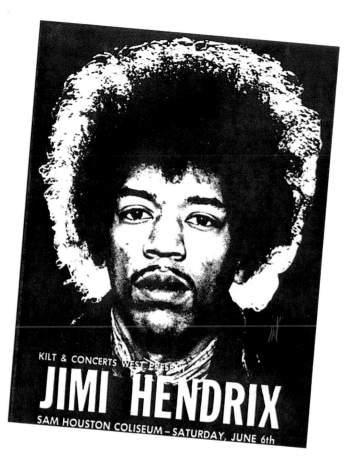

◀ **Great shot taken at the Will Rogers Coliseum, Fort Worth, Texas.**

*9 May 1970*

▲ **Jimi played two great sets in Hawaii during the so-called 'Rainbow Bridge Vibratory Color/Sound Experiment', but the resulting movie was a very poor affair.**

*30 July 1970*

◀ **Photo taken from Jimi's final Swedish concert at the Stora Scenen/Liseberg in Göteborg (with roadie Eric Barrett as spectator).**
*1 September 1970*

kr. 65.00   incl. moms

**K.B.-HALLEN**

BENDIX MUSIC
præsenterer

**JIMI HENDRIX**

torsdag 3. septbr. 1970

kl. 19

| Indgang | Gruppe |
|---------|--------|
| **D** | **19** |
| Garderobe | til venstre |

3 række nr. **25**

**4. 5. 6. SEPT. FEHMARN**

JIMI HENDRIX   TEN YEARS AFTER   TASTE   GINGER BAKER'S AIR FORCE   CANNED HEA

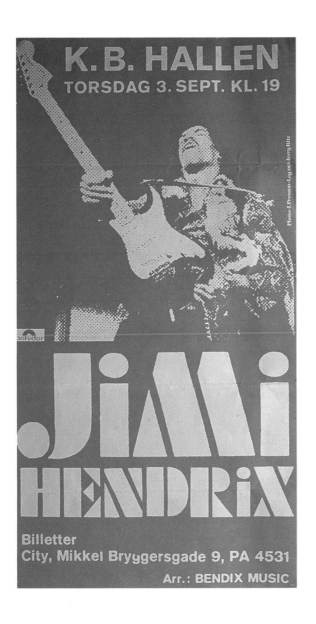

▶ Concert poster for Fehmarn. Another copy of this rather scarce poster changed hands for £4,370 during an auction at Sotheby's, London, on 14 September 1994.

▼ Extremely rare car display sticker for the Fehmarn festival.

▲ **The Isle of Fehmarn, Germany – Jimi's
final official concert performance.**
*6 September 1970*

# CHRONOLOGY

## 1942
**27 November** – Jimi is born is Seattle, named Johnny Allen Hendrix by his mother, Lucille.

## 1946
**11 September** – Jimi is renamed James Marshall Hendrix by his father, Al.

## 1951
**17 December** – Jimi's parents get divorced, and Al Hendrix gets custody of Jimi.

## 1958
**2 February** – Lucille Hendrix dies from a haemorrhage.

## 1958
Jimi gets a second-hand acoustic guitar bought by Al for $5 from a friend.

## 1959
Jimi obtains his first electric guitar, a Supro Ozark, from Myers Music Store in Seattle.

## 1959
Jimi joins his first proper band, the Rocking Kings.

## 1961
**31 May** – Jimi signs up for three years in the army.

## 1962
**January** – Jimi forms the King Casuals with Billy Cox on bass.

**2 July** – Jimi is discharged from the army on medical grounds.

## 1963
Jimi records with Lonnie Youngblood.

## 1964
**March** – Jimi joins the Isley Brothers in New York City.

## 1965
**January** – Jimi joins Little Richard's band and plays with him for about six months.

## 1966
**June/July** – Jimi forms his own band, Jimmy James and the Blue Flames.

**24 September** – Jimi arrives in London with Chas Chandler.

**1 October** – Jimi jams with Cream at the Polytechnic of Central London.

**6 October** – Jimi forms the Jimi Hendrix Experience with Noel Redding on bass and Mitch Mitchell on drums.

**12 October** – The Jimi Hendrix Experience make their debut at the Olympia in Paris supporting Johnny Hallyday.

**16 December** – 'Hey Joe' b/w 'Stone Free' released in England, the first release of the Jimi Hendrix Experience.

## 1967
**31 March** – opening date of the first Jimi Hendrix Experience UK tour at London's Astoria, sharing the bill with six other acts including the Walker Brothers, Cat Stevens and headline act Engelbert Humperdinck.

**12 May** – *Are You Experienced?*, the first Jimi Hendrix Experience album, is released in England.

**18 June** – The Jimi Hendrix Experience play at the Monterey International Pop Festival.

**8 July** – The Jimi Hendrix Experience briefly tour America as support to the Monkees.

**25 September** – The Jimi Hendrix Experience play at a 'Guitar-In' concert at the Royal Albert Hall with Bert Jansch and Paco Peña.

**14 November** – The Jimi Hendrix Experience begin their first headline tour at the Royal Albert Hall, London, supported by six other acts including Pink Floyd.

**1 December** – *Axis: Bold As Love*, the second Jimi Hendrix Experience album, is released in England.

## 1968
**February to April** – The Jimi Hendrix Experience tour in the USA and Canada.

**6 July** – The Jimi Hendrix Experience headline the Woburn Music Festival in Bedfordshire, UK.

**July to December** – The Jimi Hendrix Experience return to the USA for more concerts.

**25 October** – *Electric Ladyland*. the third Jimi Hendrix Experience album, is released in England.

## 1969
**29 June** – The Jimi Hendrix Experience play their final conert together in Denver, Colorado.

**18 August** – Jimi plays at the Woodstock Music And Art Fair in New York state with a six piece line-up called Gypsy Sun and Rainbows.

**October** – Jimi disbands Gypsy Sun and Rainbows and forms Band of Gypsys with Billy Cox on bass and Buddy Miles on drums.

**31 December** – Band of Gypsys make their debut at the Fillmore East in New York City, the first of two nights at this venue. Both nights were recorded and partly used for the *Band Of Gypsys* album.

## 1970
**25 April** – opening date of the Cry Of Love tour in Los Angeles with Billy Cox on bass and Mitch Mitchell on drums.

**30 May** – Jimi plays two shows at the Berkeley Community Theatre in Berkeley, both shows being filmed, resulting in the video release *Jimi Plays Berkeley*.

**4 July** – Jimi plays at the Atlanta Pop festival.

**30 July** – Jimi plays at the Rainbow Bridge Vibratory Color/Sound Experiment concert on the Island of Maui, Hawaii.

**30 August** – Jimi plays at the Isle of Wight Festival in England.

**6 September** – Jimi plays at the 'Love And Peace Festival' on the Isle Of Fehmarn, Germany, his last official concert.

**18 September** – Jimi is taken to St Mary Abbots Hospital in London and is pronounced dead on arrival.

**1 October** – Jimi is buried in Renton, Washington, USA.

# INDEX

# PHOTO CREDITS

Page

1 Fiona Adams/Retna (Hotel Garden, Nottingham, England, April 1967)

3 *Top Middle* : Ray Stevenson/Retna ('Marquee', London, 2 March 1967)

3 *Top Right* : Polydor (London, February/March 1967)

3 *Bottom* : Stuart K. Richman/LFI (Jimi's Flat, London, May 1967)

7 *Top* : A1 Hendrix Collection

7 *Bottom* : A1 Hendrix Collection

8 *Top* : A1 Hendrix Collection

9 *Top* : A1 Hendrix Collection

14 *Top* : Caesar Glebbeek Collection

16 Caesar Glebbeek Collection

19 Günter Zint

20 Günter Zint

21 Bruce Fleming/Rex Features

22 Petra Niemeier/Redferns

23 Ulrich Handl

24/5 Günter Zint

33 Dezo Hoffman/Rex Features

41 *Top* : David Magnus/Rex Features

41 *Bottom* : Petra Niemeier /Redferns

43 Glenn A. Baker Archives /Redferns

44/5 King Collection/Retna

47 Lampard/Jean Louis Rancurel Archives

51 Napier Russell

52 Bruce Fleming/Rex Features

61 Bildservice

62 Bildservice

64 Elliott Landy/Redferns

67 Roberto Bonanzi Collection

68/9 Stuart K. Richman/LFI

70 Stuart K. Richman/LFI

80 Jan Persson

81 *Top* : Caesar Glebbeek

82 Caesar Glebbeek

84 Michael Walmsley

85 Nash The Slash

86 Bildservice

88 Jim Cummins/Starfile

90 Henry Diltz/Retna

92 Grant H. Reid

93 Grant H. Reid

95 Joe Sia/Starfile

103 Owe Nilsson/Pressens Bild

106 Gray Knowles Collection

107 Richard Peters

111 Joe Sia

115 A1 Hendrix Collection

119 *Top* : Jan Persson

119 *Bottom Left* : Caesar Glebbeek Collection

119 *Bottom Right* : David Butcher

131 King Collection/Retna

151 LFI

180/1 Gunter Zint

196 Jean Louis Rancurel

197 BMS Platt

198 Jean Louis Rancurel

199 *Top* : Günter Zint

199 *Bottom Left* : Günter Zint

199 *Bottom Right* : Klaus Achterberg

200 Bildservice

201 *Top* : Jean Louis Rancurel

202 *Top Left* : Caesar Glebbeek

202 *Top Right* : LFI

203 Elliott Landy/Redferns

204 Nash The Slash

205 Eric Bachmann

206 Joe Sia

207 Joe Sia

208 *Top* : Bildservice

208 *Bottom* : Jan Persson

209 *Top* : Diego Tremonti

209 *Bottom* : Gary Knowles Collection

210 Grant H. Reid

211 Joe Sia

212 Thomas Yeates

213 *Top Left* : Carl Dunn

213 *Top Right* : Robert F. Peters

213 *Bottom Left* : Jim Sweeney

214 Bildservice

216 Redferns

221 Caesar Glebbeek ('Ahoy Hallen', Rotterdam, Holland - autographed at the Rheinhalle Dusseldorf, Germany, 12 January 1969)

222/3 Owe Nilsson/Pressens Bild

# ACKNOWLEDGEMENTS

### Author Acknowledgements

It would have been impossible to present so much diverse memorabilia in this book without the generous help of other Hendrix collectors around the world. So, merci to Mike Anderson, Francis Andreani, Roberto Bonanzi, Rory Campbell, Carsten Christensen, Mick Coyne, Stephen Goldsmith, Pete Harker, Torben Juel, Gary Knowles, and Jean-Yves Moguerou. I would also like to thank Joel J. Brattin, David Butcher, Al Hendrix, Karsten Laybourn, Don Leslie, Michael Madsen, Yazid Manou, Jan Persson and Nash The Slash. A very special thanks must go out to my friend Peter Herzig for his contributions to this book and for allowing me access to his extensive record and CD collection. Long may you collect 'em!

—*Caesar Glebbeek*